SSAS Pension Legacy

Build a Wealth and Personal Legacy with a SSAS Pension

by Richard Parker

Research by Richard Parker

Cover Design by James Thompson

Email: Richard.parker@SSASpensionlegacy.co.uk

Website: www.SSASpensionlegacy.co.uk

The right of Richard Parker to be identified as the author of this work has been asserted in accordance with 77 and 78 of the Copyright Design and Patents Act 1988.

ISBN 978-1-8381632-0-4

Printed in England.

Dedication

I would like to dedicate this book to my wife Pauline for the support she has given over all the years we have been together, and my two daughters, Hayley and Kelly who have given me unending love throughout their life.

The copious, and perhaps almost unhealthy, levels of tea and coffee that Pauline supplied to me whilst I was writing this book in the summerhouse at the end of our garden I will always remember. I could often be found in there at 5AM beavering away, and then a little while later out of the corner of my eye I would see a figure walking past the trees with a cup of tea. This figure would be my awesome wife and this process was relentless, even when it was raining. She'd come along, tea in hand, dressing-gown on covered with a rain coat and dripping wet. I couldn't have asked for anything else as a steaming cup of tea was presented to me. An amazing sight to behold…and my wife of course!

Disclaimer

The information in this book does not constitute financial or other professional advice and is general in nature. It does not take into account your specific circumstances and should not be acted on without professional advice from a suitably fully qualified and independent financial advisor who should have a full understanding of your current situation, future goals and objectives.

Although the author has made every effort to ensure that the information in this book was correct at the time of printing, the author does not assume and hereby disclaims any liability to any party for any loss, damage, or disruption caused by errors or omissions, whether such errors or omissions result from negligence, accident or any other cause.

The author is not an Independent Financial Advisor nor is he regulated in any way by the Financial Conduct Authority, and no reference should be taken in this book to suggest to the contrary.

Warning

1. High income withdrawals may not be sustainable during the deferral period.
2. Taking withdrawals may erode the capital value of the fund, especially if investment returns are poor and a high level of income is taken. This could result in a lower income if an annuity is eventually purchased.
3. The investment returns may be less than those shown in the illustrations.
4. Annuity rates may be at a worse level when annuity purchase takes place.

Financial Promotion

This book is not intended as a financial promotion for a SSAS pension in any shape or form. It has been written honestly based on the author's unqualified experience and knowledge of the product. Other financial products do exist that provide the same or similar benefits, and as already stated, you should and must seek guidance from suitably qualified Independent Financial Advisors for any financial products and services based on your personal and financial situation.

Contents

Chapter 1

Introduction

Pensions are a subject that make most people's eyes glaze over.... until they suddenly become important and tangible to them.

I was fortunate that at the very start of my career, my corporate employer deducted money from my earnings to put into the company pension scheme as soon as I turned 18. When I turned 55 I realised how amazing this exercise was, it was money that to be honest I never saw or missed as it was deducted at source. It then built up over time to create a financial windfall that (thanks to pension rule changes) I could take at 55 if I wished.

My interest in pensions was suddenly ignited when, nearing 55 I was approached by a financial advisor who worked for a pension specialist firm. He contacted me via LinkedIn and enquired what I intended to do with my pension. At the time, my thought was that I would simply take the monthly pension payment when I was ready to as that's what everyone did...didn't they? Well no, as I was to find out. I was asked if I had considered getting a surrender value for my pension and transferring it into a SIPP (Self Invested Personal Pension – more on this in Chapter 2)? Again, I had no idea what this chap was talking about – surrender value for my pension, what was this all about? It was following several conversations with him that I realised two key things if I stayed with my corporate pension scheme:

1. When I die, my pension payments are reduced by 50% to my wife.

2. When she dies, my pension fund (my money!) goes back into the company pension scheme to pay out to other employees' pension payments regardless of how much I've paid in (or how little I'd received depending on how quickly I died). In this situation nothing is left to go to my now grown up children and this is generally how all occupational

pension funds work.

So the sales pitch was that if I transferred my pension from my corporate employer scheme, I could put it into a pension 'vehicle', but the key thing was that when I die the whole fund is still there (less any drawings I have made) for my wife to access. When she dies, the pension pot is again still all there for my children to access (with some restrictions explained later in the book). It doesn't go anywhere and there is no percentage reduction – it would be fully intact.

This was a real lightbulb moment for me....and it should be for you!

This also reminded me of an event that happened early in my career when I was about 19 as an apprentice and working in the Engine Plant at Dagenham for Ford Motor Company. We had an engine testing area where there was a group of dynamometer cells that test engines, taking them through various cycles, and these were run to check the engines performance by skilled operators. These operators had been employed for many, many years but a group of them all retired together. I seem to recall there were about 8 of them in total that left at about the same time, but sadly within a year to 18 months of them leaving, 5 of them had died. This came as a real shock to everyone at work and I remember vowing at the time I would never end up in that situation i.e. die a few years after retiring, I needed to plan to retire as early as possible.

I should separately point out at this juncture that unfortunately, if you are employed in the public sector in the UK, there is no pot to transfer.

In the public sector (and the basic State Pension where you must have paid or been credited with National Insurance contributions) it's basically like a massive pyramid scheme although it's obviously not fraudulent. What I mean is that that new employees or the general UK labour force get deducted money (National Insurance) which pays out to pensioners when they reach a certain age (which is gradually increasing due to people living longer). If the number of pensioners increase beyond those paying in, you get a gap and that's why the government must keep growing worker numbers (hence immigration) or reducing pension pay-outs (cue riots in the streets like those happening in France at the time of writing for this exact reason) or deferring pay-outs by saying you don't get a pension till you are 67, 70, 75 etc. which is exactly what we are seeing in Britain today. So, if you are employed in the public sector (NHS, teacher, council worker, army etc.) or in a blue light service in the UK, there is no pot available to move into a SSAS (Small Self-Administered Scheme) – it doesn't exist because of the funding scheme approach, sorry...

Now, going back to me, at the time I was approached by this financial advisor, I was fully employed running a business as its Managing Director and hadn't even considered my pension for years. However, thanks to this contact from the financial advisor and good old George Osbourne (a previous Chancellor of the Exchequer), I was reminded and further informed that if I wanted to I could:

1. Access my pension from the age of 55 and,

2. Move the pension fund I had built up somewhere else like a SIPP or a SSAS if I wanted to.

I had invested in shares in the past and had always lost money. I even had a private pension SIPP (set up and paid into regularly after I left my large corporate employer after 24 years) that was managed for me and invested in the stock market and when I looked at the balance of my fund in 2017, guess what – it was worth less than what I had paid in. Shares had not worked out well for me and as I already had a SIPP, I certainly wasn't going to create a new one just so a financial advisor could take a great big fat fee for managing this all for me and losing even more of my money all over again.

It was at this time I started to hear about something called a SSAS pension.

I knew nothing about it but I had heard people talking about this type of pension in some property forums and podcasts, although it seemed to be shrouded in mystery. Little did I know these had been around for many, many years (in excess of 40) and were mainly used historically by business owners who ran their business from a commercial building that they owned. This is why a SSAS is also often referred to as a Directors Pension. But now I was starting to hear about people who were buying property with their SSAS funds and renting out the building with the rental income going into their SSAS pot which would obviously build up over time. Even if you only got a 6-7% return per annum on your pension (which is the same amount that Warren Buffett believes the stock market returns as an average[1]), your pension pot is still growing and you are in complete control of it.

This really piqued my interest and I immediately thought, I know I'll go out and buy a load of residential property to add to my rental portfolio (which I had been running as a side gig to my main career for about 13 years)…but I quickly realised HMRC had put the brakes on anything like that by the imposition of huge fines if you did any such thing. But I was to discover there are a lot of ways to utilise your SSAS funds to help your pension pot grow but again many of these methods seemed shrouded in mystery and getting to fully understand what you needed to do to ensure you didn't fall foul of HMRC's rules was far from easy.

The thing about a SSAS pension is that it is potentially a fantastic tool to allow you to leave a wealth legacy to your nearest and dearest. However, it could be the case that you may not be so focussed on wealth creation for yourself…. maybe you want to leave some kind of social legacy that improves society even just a little bit, or perhaps a legacy that will help save the planet if you wish. Using a SSAS pension can potentially be a great enabler for you to use for improving all kinds of things. This is possible through its ability to release capital that's normally locked up in a pension fund. The sums that can be released could be truly life changing either for you, your family or for people you don't even know yet.

Before I go any further, let's get the disclaimer out of the way.

I'm not a financial advisor nor am I 'regulated by the Financial Services Authority' and your risk profile, circumstances, motivations and world view are likely to be completely different to mine. You MUST and need to do your own research and speak to suitably qualified advisors on the topics raised in this book. Please do not take the information contained in this book to be in any way competent financial advice. The idea of this book is that it will hopefully spark an interest in SSAS pensions for you. If it does, then you need to go and speak to a financial professional because I am certainly not one in such matters. To be clear, you read and act on the following at your own risk.

So, there you are, you have been warned.

I decided to write this book after initially just wanting to educate myself fully on what opportunities were available for investment using a SSAS pension, what I needed to do in each case and to build up a list of case studies to understand more fully what was needed to be implemented in each situation. Initially my research on the ways you could invest using a SSAS was for my own education, but I quickly realised that such knowledge would probably benefit a lot of other people as well. So I decided to write this book to bring together lots of the scattered information that is available on the internet together in one place. I would show everyone how to use a SSAS pension and share it with people who may be equally interested in how to make the most of it to build their own wealth.

Because of my interest in property and being a portfolio landlord, I have primarily focused on property related case studies in this book. There are other things you can do with your SSAS in terms of investment that are purely financially related, but that is not of great interest to me and frankly beyond what I wanted to cover in this book. I do cover some of these in the book but not being very experienced in such things, I will leave you to speak to specialists regarding these investment vehicles. That said it is extremely prudent to diversify some of your investments so you don't have all your eggs in one basket e.g. property.

If you have an interest in using property and using a SSAS to grow your wealth, I hope you find this book and the case studies of interest. Once you settle on a preferred route please don't however use this book as a 'playbook' as it's beyond this content to cover every avenue you could go down. But for each given case study, it should and will give you a good overview of the approach and what is needed. Then having understood it as much as possible, that's the time to speak to specialist experts like accountants, tax advisors, solicitors etc. and they will help ensure you follow the rules. Actually, you may well find you know more than your accountant, tax advisor (unless they are specifically a property tax advisor) or solicitor does. If that's the case, maybe you need to find a new one that specialises in this field.

Each chapter will start with an explanation of how you can invest your SSAS fund in a particular way. This will be followed in most cases by one or two case study examples on how you can utilise your SSAS funds in the method described.

Now I found an interesting thing happened when I contacted people in my network about their own use of SSAS investments. Whilst many were happy to share their experience of how they had invested using theirs or others SSAS funds, getting them to agree to be named in this book was incredibly difficult. Now I think this is down to three reasons:

Firstly, no doubt there is a natural reluctance for revealing any more than necessary to HMRC, but I think it is also the fact that they will not generally sanction advice in advance, or very rarely give this advice in advance…..especially not without wanting 'war and peace' on the investment. You therefore are forced to make a decision on your investment (with your scheme administrator and other advisors) and HMRC will then decide if it's acceptable or not when they become aware of it. Yes, they provide guidelines on what is and is not an acceptable investment, but they could decide what you've invested in (or the way you've done it) does not follow this guidance or the rules.

Secondly, SSAS pensions are becoming more and more popular. This means that some people are seeking 'creative' ways to use their pension funds and are perhaps pushing the boundaries of what is and is not acceptable. This could be in some part driven by a lack of clarity in some areas from HMRC, clarity that often only gets resolved from a legal test case being brought, and few want to be the guinea pig for a certain strategy going to court.

Thirdly, professional SSAS administrators/advisors sometimes give different advice. One will say investment type 'A' is acceptable, whilst another professional advisor will say 'A' is not acceptable because they have interpreted the HMRC guidelines differently.

So, as a result of the above three points, I have had to change the names in a number of instances. By the way, if you want to read all of the real nitty, gritty details about a SSAS pension, it's all contained in the scores of pages in the Pension Tax Manual – PTM120000 which is updated regularly (usually monthly but this is mostly formatting updates or similar) and can be found on the 'gov.uk' website[2].

Now, regardless of what you purchase or secure as an investment, be this property, land, shares etc., due diligence is an important aspect of any investment.

Due diligence is loosely defined as an investigation, audit, or review performed to confirm the facts of a matter under consideration. In the context of a SSAS investment, due diligence will likely require an examination of financial and legal records before entering into a proposed transaction with another party.

This is so important I've dedicated a whole section (Chapter 3) to explain what this is and how to go about it when considering a SSAS investment. Remember, this is your pension and you probably worked (or will work) your whole life for it. Don't fritter it away simply because you were lazy in conducting some research about an investment.

Before we get into the content properly, one request – please scribble lots of notes in the book (or separate notes if you are using a kindle version), circle points and bend down the corners of pages where there are important sections in them, which are relevant to you, mark them. Use this book as a tool, it is here to be used and not left sitting on the shelf. Come back to it as your understanding grows and make more notes and comments. I do this with most of my reference books so I don't have to go through the pages again and find an important section. I hope you'll do the same.

If you are listening to the audible version of this book, hopefully you've turned your car into a 'university' and you should have a voice recorder in your car to record voice memos – but obviously not while you're driving.

Right, so let's get into the detail and explain exactly what a SSAS pension is and how you can use it to invest in yours and your descendant's future.

Chapter 2

SSAS Pension and What You Can Invest In

Initially I will explain what a SSAS pension is, the potential benefits of having one and what it can and can't invest in. Then we will explain a simple process for setting up a SSAS if you don't already have one in place.

What is a SSAS pension?

A Small Self-Administered Scheme (SSAS) is an occupational pension scheme which is subject to the normal rules and regulations for registered pension schemes whilst offering flexibility over the types of investment it can make. They are generally set up to provide retirement benefits for a small number of a company's directors and the most senior or key staff. The pension can be open to all employees and their family members over the age of 18, even if they don't work for the employer. The number of members allowed must be no more than eleven. A SSAS is run by its Trustees, a scheme administrator (which can be an external professional company and/or one of the trustees performing this role) who are often also members of the scheme, but this type of scheme is limited to one SSAS pension per company.

Contributions can be made to the SSAS by the members and/or the employers. On this basis each receives tax relief on the contributions made, obviously subject to certain conditions.

SSAS pensions are not uncommon in small or family-run businesses and are a type of defined contribution pension scheme. HMRC SSAS rules allow members to invest in a range of assets (more on the types of investments allowed later). The scheme can also offer loans on a commercial basis and can therefore provide a loan to the sponsoring company (again, more on this later) in order to purchase an asset such as a new commercial building. A further difference of this kind of scheme is that it can borrow money (via a mortgage for example) as long as it's for investment purposes.

There are also generous tax concessions afforded to a SSAS which are advantageous to both a company and its directors. These can be used to develop a highly effective and coordinated approach to minimising corporate and personal taxation, with contributions possible by the members and/or the employer. Each receives tax relief on contributions made, subject to certain conditions.

What are the advantages?

An advantage of a SSAS is that it can offer potentially increased flexibility on where the scheme's funds can be invested. This can include investing in assets that aren't generally available for many other types of scheme to invest in. One of the main opportunities available, and one that is commonly employed by business owners, is where a SSAS is able to purchase the company's trading premises and lease these back to the company. As already stated, subject to certain terms and conditions, it is able to lend money back to the company and purchase the company's shares.

A SSAS can also borrow money, subject to terms and conditions, for investment purposes. For example, the SSAS may raise a mortgage to assist with the purchase of the company's premises by the scheme and the mortgage repayments can then be covered by the rental income that the company pays into the SSAS. All of the SSAS's assets are held in the name of the Trustees. This means there are individual pots for each member, although each member does effectively hold a proportion of the scheme's assets.

When can I draw the benefits?

The earliest you can start drawing benefits from the SSAS is from the age of 55 (the minimum age is expected to increase to 57 from 2028 with further increases as the state pension age goes up[3]). There is now no upper age limit by which retirement benefits must be taken. There are no restrictions on people's ability to draw down from their defined contribution pension pots after age 55. The value of your benefits from the SSAS will depend on a number of things such as how much has been paid into the scheme on your behalf, the length of time that each contribution has been invested, investment growth over this period and the level of charges the scheme has incurred.

Generally, you can decide whether to receive an income only from the scheme, or a tax-free cash lump sum as well as an income. Taking a lump sum will reduce your regular income as a result. The amount of tax-free cash sum that you can elect to take is usually up to a maximum of 25% of the value of your pension pot under the SSAS at retirement. The balance of the fund is then used to provide income through other means such as purchasing an annuity (this is where you make a lump-sum payment to an insurance company and, in return, receive regular payments back) by income drawdown (this means leaving your pension money invested and taking cash as and when you need it), or a pension paid directly by the SSAS from its assets (scheme pension).

The amount of income you will receive will depend on a number of decisions that you will have taken. These will include:

- Whether you want the income to be continued to be paid to a dependant should you die.
- Increasing the amount of income you receive each year to offset the effects of inflation based on your investment decisions.
- The frequency at which the income is paid i.e. in chunks or on a regular monthly payment.

Pensions payments that are paid are liable to Income Tax (this varies from 0% to 45% currently depending on your income), but are not liable to National Insurance contributions.

If you've previously contributed to several other pension schemes, you may have retained benefits under that scheme. In this case you may want to consider transferring the value of any old pensions to your SSAS pension scheme, to consolidate all the funds in one place. But be aware there is a limit on the amount of pension benefits you can draw, known as the 'lifetime allowance'.

What is the Lifetime Allowance?

This is a limit on the amount of pension benefit that can be drawn from pension schemes – whether lump sums or retirement income – and can be paid without triggering an extra tax charge. If the total value of your pension benefits exceeds the lifetime allowance the excess benefit will be subject to a tax charge of up to 55%.

The lifetime allowance for the tax year 2020/21 is £1,073,100 and it is likely to increase in line with inflation[4]. It may be possible to keep a higher lifetime allowance if one of the forms of protection is already held or applied for:

- Individual Protection 2016 (IP2016) – on the 5th April 2016, if you had total pension savings in excess of £1million, this protection is available to you. If you meet certain criteria, individuals can fix their lifetime allowance at the value of their pension fund on this date – to a maximum of £1.25 million. Funding of your pension can continue with further funding likely to be conditional to a lifetime allowance charge.

- Fixed Protection 2016 - fixes an individual's lifetime allowance to protect their pension savings at £1.25m after 5 April 2016 when the lifetime allowance dropped from £1.25m to £1m. It fixes the individual's lifetime allowance at £1.25 million but doesn't allow any further pension funding after 5th April 2016.

While most people aren't affected by the lifetime allowance, you should take action if the value of your pension benefits is approaching, or above, the lifetime allowance. It may be necessary to stop contributing to your SSAS even though you have not retired, to avoid your benefits exceeding the lifetime allowance. Personal and specific advice is recommended in this area before making any decisions.

How is a SSAS different from a SIPP?

In very general terms, a SSAS is a pension scheme for (commonly small) employers and a SIPP is a pension scheme for an individual.

No doubt quite a few of you will have heard of SIPP or may even have one, and there are a number of differences between a SSAS and a SIPP[5]. The main one includes a SSAS being able to make a loan to a sponsoring employer – this is often referred to as a 'loanback' (more on this in Chapter 7).

Whereas a loan from a SIPP to a connected party is normally treated as an unauthorised payment and subject to heavy tax charges, with a SSAS up to 50% of the fund can be loaned to the sponsoring employer of the scheme. Such a loan obviously has to meet certain requirements in relation to the security and repayment terms, but it can be potentially one way to fund capital expenditure for the business. This could also possibly provide a valuable and tax efficient investment return for the pension scheme members.

The cost of a SSAS is more expensive to set up, but having multiple members starts to even out the fees compared to a SIPP[6]. Market competition is also likely to be reduce these fees over time. Another difference I would say there is between a SIPP and a SSAS is that you need to run your SSAS like a business. Whereas a SIPP could potentially be a relatively hands-off investment (in my humble opinion), a SSAS should absolutely not be a hands-off investment process (even if you are investing in hands-off assets). You need to review its performance regularly and take appropriate action as required. If you have a corporate pension and are quite happy to just check your statement once a year from your employer, frown but then simply put it in the drawer and not think about it again, a SSAS is possibly not for you.

What can my SSAS invest in?

Here we are starting to get into the detail of what it is possible to do with the funds in a SSAS and the amazing benefits that can come from it.

If we focus on property for a moment, acceptable properties must be commercial, located in the UK and can be either freehold (outright ownership of the property) or leasehold (holding property for a specific number of years in return for paying a rent to the landlord).

Acceptable commercial property includes:

- Office buildings - which are a common investment.
- Industrial/business units and warehouses.
- Shops.
- Agricultural or commercial land or forestry.
- Land for commercial development.
- Garages.
- Nursing homes.
- Public houses.
- Marine berths.
- Student accommodation – this must be student halls attached to the university, not a HMO (house of multiple occupancy).
- Hotels (this could potentially include serviced accommodation (SA), but this is precarious ground for investment so be careful and read the next paragraph).

Referencing serviced accommodation which is a very popular investment these days, if it were a bed & breakfast for example of 10+ units and C1 status then that is clearly a commercial use class and technically would be acceptable. However, if it were a 2 bedroomed semi-detached former residential house 'badged' as service accommodation, then that very clearly would not be an acceptable purchase. HMRC will likely look at the building itself and if it is clearly a residential building, then they will consider it residential for SSAS purposes, even if it's being operated as SA (regardless of council rates) and so an investment would be considered an unauthorised payment.

The acceptability of any commercial property should be subject to satisfactory due diligence by you and your advisors. Also, it's worth noting that non-permanent fixtures and fittings must be excluded from the property purchase otherwise they could give rise to a tax charge.

Commercial property can be developed or refurbished as part of a pension scheme provided that no residential element is added. Similarly, land can be purchased and used to develop commercial premises. Again, you should undertake due diligence with your advisors to review the proposals so you can be sure they meet HMRC's rules prior to any work taking place. If you or a connected person's business (see below) is to undertake the property development/refurbishment, you should obtain quotes from that business along with independent quotes from at least two other unconnected businesses for comparison purposes. You can of course also purchase commercial property at auction through your SSAS pension scheme and you can develop the property that it holds.

Other things you can invest in include the funds in most types of conventional investments such as:

- Regulated Collective Investments such as Unit Trusts, OEICS and ICVCs.

- Gilts and fixed interest stocks.

- Investment trusts - these are equity investment funds generally managed by insurance companies.

- Direct quoted equities - the typical stocks and shares found in most standard pension funds.

- Trustee investment plans.

- Hedge funds - these are pooled investments generally made by financial institutions, such as insurance companies and banks.

- Gold - investing in investment grade gold bullion (subject to conditions).

- NS&I - National Savings and Investments include Income Bonds with easy access.

- Loanback to the principal employer (see Chapter 7).

- Commercial loans - this includes both secured and unsecured loans to UK limited companies (see Chapter 8).

At this point it's worth mentioning something called 'connected persons' as this has some aspects that you need to be aware of for any investments you make.

Your pension scheme can purchase property from you, a person connected with you or any other party. However, any purchase from or disposal (including a lease) to a connected person must be evidenced as being on a commercial basis. It needs to be on something referred to as 'arm's length terms' (this is where buyers and sellers act independently without one party influencing the other). This can be demonstrated via an independent professional property valuation by a recognised RICS (Royal Institution of Chartered Surveyors) surveyor who is a registered valuer. They will carry out the valuation in accordance with RICS 'Red Book' standards (which contains mandatory rules, best practice guidance and related commentary for all RICS members undertaking asset valuations).

A connected person consists of:

- You (as the member).
- Your spouse or civil partner.
- Your relatives for you as a member.
- The relatives of your spouse.
- Any person who is in a partnership with you or your spouse or civil partner or relative.
- A company whose actions you direct e.g., you are the business director, or a person connected with you.

In this situation, a brother, sister or similar descendent will be considered a relative. There needs to be an 'arm's length' commercial arrangement for any rental payments between connected parties so there is no risk of tax charges being applied. Remember the rental liability will still continue even if a tenant is a connected party and is in financial difficulty. In other words, you will need to pursue payment by legal means just as if they were not connected.

I've tried to make the details previously mentioned as inclusive as possible but I cannot guarantee the list is exhaustive, and it's worth noting that not all SSAS providers will allow investment into each of these options, so it is important to check the rules of your SSAS provider before attempting to invest your pension.

So this all sounds potentially amazing doesn't it, unfortunately there are some things you can't do regarding SSAS investments…well no one said you'd found the holy grail of investments but it's not that bad.

What must I not invest in?

There are also some restrictions imposed by HMRC designed solely to prevent abuse and it is very important you are aware of these.

Generally, if your SSAS holds what is considered to be prohibited assets (the most obvious one being residential property) either directly or indirectly, it will lose its tax advantages. What this broadly means is that, at the minimum, there is no more advantage in holding such an asset in a pension scheme than there is in holding it personally.

Concentrating on property for the moment, it is absolutely clear no residential property is allowed – this is a fundamental rule!

Having stated that quite clearly, an element of residential living is actually permitted in a few exceptional circumstances. This would be where you have a commercial property and there is a need for a residential element being essential for its operation (see Chapter 6 for more details on this). However, the employee cannot be connected to any pension scheme member (see the list for connected persons mentioned earlier) and any rent paid will need to be on a commercial basis.

You should also not invest in land that is or was attached to a residential property (unless it already has planning for a commercial property). Convincing HMRC that buying a piece of your garden because you think you can put a commercial building on it, for example, is potentially risky to say the least. In this instance you should probably get planning permission first before even considering buying it with your SSAS funds.

Other non-acceptable properties include:

- Holiday lets.
- Timeshares.

- Beach huts.
- Commercial freeholds where there is also a reversionary interest in a residential leasehold within the property (which means you, or rather your SSAS, has the right to buy the residential element of the property when the lease ends).
- Student flats (unless as already mentioned they are part of a hall of residence directly connected to an educational establishment).

Additional to the above regarding property, if a pension scheme is involved in regular property buying and/or developing and selling, HMRC may find such transactions as 'trading.' Whilst both capital and income investment gains are normally tax exempt, if trading is considered to apply to your SSAS pension, any associated income and capital gains would then be taxed accordingly… so no trading!

Other prohibited assets include such things as:

- Fine wines.
- Classic cars (boo! …will I ever find a way to fund buying an AC Cobra?).
- Art & antiques.

Again, this list of prohibited assets is not exhaustive.

If you find yourself in the unfortunate position where your SSAS directly or indirectly purchases a prohibited asset, the purchase will be considered by HMRC to be an "unauthorised member payment" and subject to charges. Whilst I have been told that HMRC will try to work out such situations with you and your advisors, I suggest you don't find yourself in such an unfortunate position as you could end up with nothing less than a massive tax charge.

That's why it's so important not to find yourself in this situation as HMRC will/could look to recover all the tax relief given on the amounts used to purchase the asset and much more. What this actually would mean is that the following charges could apply:

- Unauthorised payment charge - the member will be subject to an income tax charge at 40% on the value of the prohibited asset or unauthorised payment.

- Unauthorised payment surcharge - if the total unauthorised payments from the SSAS exceeds 25% of the SSAS assets in any twelve-month period, the recipient of the payments may be liable for a further free-standing charge of 15% of the surchargeable payments i.e. the value of the asset.

- Surcharge - if the value of the prohibited asset exceeds 25% of the value of the pension scheme's assets in any 12-month period, the scheme may be de-registered which would lead to a tax charge on the scheme administrator on the value of the scheme assets at the rate of 40%.

So, as you can see, absolutely terrifying levels of tax charges.

Having set up your SSAS correctly and invested wisely increasing its value over time, you are likely to start thinking about what happens to the fund when you eventually pass on to the 'next level' or 'plane of enlightenment' (very Buddhist I know) and you are no longer of this world.

Death Payments

What a depressing title for a section but that said, this is one of the best advantages about having a SSAS, and that is that the value of the pension fund remains intact and is available to your beneficiaries on your death (this is also true of a SIPP). It can normally be withdrawn as a lump sum or left within the pension wrapper to be drawn on to provide a regular income. Death benefits, whether drawn as a lump sum or income, are normally payable tax free to your beneficiaries if you die before the age of 75.

Now to be very serious for a moment, consider this very important fact if you are in seriously poor health. No one can obviously predict when they will die but if you have a serious illness and consider that dying before the age of 75 is a real possibility, leaving your pension pot in a SSAS absolutely tax free to your next of kin is a real kindness to those you leave behind should the worst happen.

Hopefully we are all in absolutely the peak of good health so if you die after the age of 75, death benefits withdrawn as income or a lump sum are taxable on the recipients as earned income....but no doubt this is one kind of tax that we all hope to be paying by having a long life.

The only death benefits assessed against the lifetime pension allowance will be those available from uncrystallised funds (i.e. funds from which you have not yet drawn at all) either as lump sums or in flexi-access drawdown from death before age 75. If those benefits exceed your remaining lifetime allowance, if taken as a lump sum or placed in flexi-access drawdown, there will be a tax charge on the excess.

Now, no doubt having gone through the details so far, you are beginning to understand some of the potential advantages of utilising a SSAS for your retirement planning. Well, not just anyone can have a SSAS pension, at least not without going through some hoops to make it happen and become eligible.

SSAS Eligibility

So assuming first of all you are not a public sector employee (the reasons for this already explained in my introduction in Chapter 1), to be eligible to invest in a SSAS and receive tax relief on personal contributions, an individual investor must be under 75 years of age and resident in the UK (there are a few exemptions but I'm not going to consider the details here).

It's also worth noting here that the costs of establishing and running a SSAS far exceed that of mainstream personal or workplace pensions and even those of a SIPP. So, to establish and use a SSAS, there has to be a valid need and reasoning to justify this extra cost before even worrying about its eligibility.

Contributions to the SSAS can be made by yourself, your sponsoring employer or even a third party e.g. a parent or spouse. Also, just to be clear, you can start contributing to your SSAS pension once you are 18 (just like any other pension).

That all sounds straightforward but as you personally will be responsible for making pension investments, there will be checks insisted upon by pension watchdogs to make sure you are capable of making such decisions. This will likely involve a lengthy interview with just such a specialist pension advisor or suitable accountant. As contributions can be made by your sponsoring employer as mentioned above, by default this means you will have (or will need to) set up a limited company business. This will probably need to have been existence for a minimum of 6 months (ideally longer) before even applying to establish the pension scheme. Remember a SSAS was and is also known as a director's pension, so the clue is in the name of why these were created. So, no business, no SSAS pension scheme.

Having determined you are eligible and in a position to establish the pension, there are some limits on the contributions which are possible to the scheme by you and others.

Contribution Limits

The minimum contribution varies between companies but typically amounts to about £20 a month and contributions can be halted at any time. Despite the many tax benefits available when it comes to funding a personal pension, there are limitations on tax-relievable contributions which can be made. Individuals may make donations of up to 100% of their yearly income, up to a certain limit. The total amount of pension contributions that each person can make without incurring a tax charge (this includes employer and employee contributions) is also limited annually. This is called the annual allowance, and is different from the previously mentioned lifetime allowance.

Annual Allowance

The Annual Allowance is the upper limit, for a tax year, on the total value of contributions paid by or for a member to the SSAS in that tax year that can benefit from tax relief. At the time of writing, this is currently £40,000 gross/year but this may change in the future, so check with your specialist advisor for the current limit. If the contribution exceeds the annual allowance, you'll have to pay a tax charge. Depending on your taxable income the excess pension savings could be charged tax in whole or in part, anything between 20% and 45%.

There are some other more complicated calculations around the annual allowance depending on some other factors which are referred to as money purchase annual allowance (this is where you've accessed pension benefits), tapered annual allowance and also where you have unused annual allowance but that is too much for this book. Again, speak to your specialist advisor on these topics.

Taxation

Donations to a pension produce direct tax benefits, and donations are made net of basic rate tax relief, meaning you are only going to directly pay £80 net for every £100 of contributions received … great! Equally, higher and additional taxpayers make donations net of base rate tax and can then receive extra relief via their tax return.

When made, the pension payments will be invested in funds where there is no tax burden on capital gains, and all qualifying types of investment income are also tax-free. An employer can contribute, and seek corporate tax relief for any amount agreed by their local tax inspector.

Types of SSAS

Now I know that's a lot of information to absorb but I'm afraid I just need to add a further complication at this stage. There are actually different types of SSAS – a defined benefit (DB) scheme and a defined contribution (DC) scheme. Much of what we cover in this book is based on a DC scheme as these are generally the most common for small family businesses who take out a SSAS, but it is worth mentioning what a DB SSAS offers before we move onto the main subject of the book.

DB schemes are advantaged in certain ways and one of the main differences is the flexibility it has to exceed the annual allowance.

The way annual payments are determined for a DB scheme is complex and dependent on the level of annuities. Nevertheless, using a DB SSAS allows you to surpass the annual benefit by the amount of contributions needed to receive the desired pension. It ensures that new members of the scheme can easily build up a large pension and can also help older clients who choose to establish a pension fund in a limited period of time or later in their career.

Let's assume you wanted to make a contribution to a DC SSAS. You are limited to £40,000 as the maximum you can invest as that's the maximum annual allowance you have. By using a DB SSAS and following some complex calculations based on retirement date, the annual allowance and any unused annual allowance, the DB SSAS would then be funded for that level of pension from the client's normal retirement date. This could possibly result in a value which is 2 or 3 times the available annual allowance[7]. Based on the standard allowance of £40,000/annum, this could then become an investment of up to £120,000 into the DB SSAS in one year. If the member has unused allowances from previous tax years, this figure can be even higher.

Well worth thinking about if you're getting towards retirement time, your business has made some seriously significant profits in a given year and you've got unused allowance. If you do find yourself in this position, it would be essential to discuss this approach with a financial professional to see if this route is suitable for your circumstances.

Now to continue with a focus on a DC SSAS.

Setting up a SSAS

Wondering how to set up a SSAS pension? Here are some things that you will need to think about to make sure your scheme is set up efficiently, simply and – most importantly – legally. It is worth pointing out that this whole process can be conducted by a specialist SSAS provider if you do not want to manage the process yourself.

I personally did, and still use, a SSAS administration company to handle all this for me as I found one that held my hand and guided me through the whole process without taking over and ordering me around like some firms seem to.

1. Decide who will be part of the scheme - your SSAS can have no more than eleven members. Normally these will be directors or senior staff from the sponsoring company that you work for. However, scheme members may also invite

family members to be part of the SSAS. Either way, the first step is to finalise who is going to be part of the SSAS.

2. Choose a scheme name – the SSAS needs an official name. You can be as creative as you like, from 'The Parker Family Pension Scheme' to 'The Nikolai Tesla AC Pension Scheme' (yes, I am a fan of this great man).

3. Appoint a scheme administrator - unless you are working with a professional SSAS provider to manage your scheme (which I highly recommend), you will need to appoint one of your members to be the scheme administrator. Their duties will involve administrative responsibilities such as fulfilling HMRC obligations and keeping other trustees informed about how the SSAS is performing.

4. Gather up the paperwork - to create your SSAS you will need to collect legal information about the sponsoring employer as well as the personal details and signatures of each member of the scheme.

5. Don't forget about anti-money laundering legislation - you have a legal obligation to comply with anti-money laundering legislation. Each member of the SSAS will need to have their identity verified.

6. Open a new bank account - you will need at least one designated bank account for the SSAS, however you can establish multiple bank accounts to serve different purposes should you wish, such as to receive contributions and to handle investment income, hold tenant deposits etc. If you are choosing not to appoint a professional trustee (scheme administrator) you may find the options for opening bank accounts limited as many banks will insist that a suitably qualified scheme trustee is in place.

7. Register your SSAS with HMRC - you must register your SSAS with HMRC before you can start to receive contributions from your members. Upon registration HMRC will give you a Pension Scheme Tax Reference

(PSTR) number - a unique code that verifies that your scheme has been registered for tax relief and exemptions. This process can take many months to complete.

8. Register with The Pensions Regulator - the UK regulator for work-based pensions. It's their job to make sure everything is above board with your pension.

9. Share explanatory information with members - you are likely to receive lots of paperwork during the SSAS registration process. This should be distributed to all members of the scheme to make sure every trustee knows what's required of them and how they can access their pension.

Once you've completed these steps you are ready to start to use the SSAS for holding pension funds. These can be through contributions or via a transfer from other existing schemes that you may want to consolidate.

What are the risks with a SSAS?

There are a number of risk considerations that need to be taken into account and probably the biggest one could be you!

You (and any fellow trustees you have) are now personally taking responsibility for your own pension funds. Unlike a corporate pension where the investment decisions are left to someone else to make, with a SSAS it's all down to you and the advisors you personally use. That said, this is one of the key reasons people do take out a SSAS – so they can make their own decisions.

Regardless, it is important that you are aware of the risks involved:

- What you will get back in terms of returns depends on how your investments grow and on the tax treatment of the investments. Some of this is and is not in your control.

- The value of your fund can obviously go down as well as up and the value will depend on how much is saved, the charges paid and the rate at which the investment grows (or loses). As always stated in such things, past performance is no guarantee of future returns. Whilst you hold more control, any positive or negative returns are clearly based on what you've invested in.

- Any employer contribution to your plan is dependent upon the continued solvency of your employer and this again is usually within your control as you are likely to be a director of the sponsoring employer.

- Depending how it is taken, your pension income may also depend on interest and annuity rates at the time you retire and these generally are not within your control.

- Some investments e.g. property may not be readily realisable (they are illiquid) and will be subject to market conditions at that time.

- This investment is intended as a long-term investment and is definitely not a get rich quick process.

- The current tax treatment and annual contribution limits may change in the future and these are clearly not within your control.

So, as you would expect with any financial investment, there are pros and cons around the investments you can make. Hopefully having reviewed these, you'll feel the pros outweigh the cons and will still believe that having a SSAS pension is the right way forward for you.

Whilst there are some risks, there is a way you can mitigate some of the risks around your investments and that is by carrying out something called Due Diligence.

Chapter 3

Due Diligence

This subject can be enormously broad, and each due diligence project differs from acquisition to acquisition. As an absolute minimum it could be considered an audit but generally it incorporates a much larger scope. You should undertake due diligence on every financial transaction you're considering but the depth and amount of due diligence you undertake will usually depend on the amount you are investing. The due diligence on a £10,000 investment is potentially likely to be a lot less than a £100,000 investment depending on your circumstances and how much these sums mean to you.

There have been many very large business failures that were apparently all regulated by the authorities e.g. Lehman Brothers, so do not assume regulation is some kind of guarantee of security or success, or that you don't have to worry about due diligence. You should always carry out due diligence on both regulated businesses and alternative opportunities.

Proper due diligence will reassure you that there is a transparent and reliable legal framework for the investment. You will know what tangible properties you will possess, how they are held and handled, and the conditions in which they can be sold or transferred. Some considerations include the obligations that you and the supplier of the assets have, the requirements that must be met and what happens if either party fails to meet them.

This often includes lawful contracts, particularly in the case of lending opportunities. It is also prudent to seek advice from your trusted professional and financial experts or wider network.

You Need Due Diligence

It doesn't matter whether you're choosing to invest your SSAS money into some kind of packaged investment, or lend it to a business or an individual, there are a number of key risks to consider:

- The asset having a lack of liquidity, meaning it might be difficult to recover your money when you need it.

- Without inside knowledge, it's often hard to value the underlying asset (this is why Warren Buffett spends so much time reading company reports).

- There's often little governance by the authorities, particularly with overseas investments which I think should generally be avoided (because of the different rules and legal structures).

- Complicated contractual terms and conditions.

- A lack of on-going information about the investment.

One of the easiest ways of carrying out due diligence is to establish whether an opportunity is worth pursuing. You do this by having the asset provider answer a series of relevant questions. Having some kind of checklist of the information needed is a good idea but the checklist will vary between different asset types so the greater the quantity of different types of investments, the more data is needed. Good quality information with supporting evidence should give you as much information as possible and where any of the questions answered give insufficient information, make sure you find out what you need to know some other way before you part with your money.

The following is a list of the typical things to consider in any investment situation:

Valuation of the Property/Asset

- The asset should be independently valued. Any asset should always be valued independently (which means someone not paid for by you or the asset holder) and banks will often ask for their own assessors to value an asset - even if you have had your own valuation carried out.

- There needs to be a clear inventory or list of what the valuation does and does not include.

Funds Usage

- It needs to be clearly stated to whom and where the funds you are paying are going too.
- A statement of what the money is being used for e.g. to allow development works to be carried out or to purchase a property.
- It needs to be clearly documented how fees, charges, marketing, salaries and costs are to be paid for.
- There should be transparency over the costs and that they are reasonable and appropriate.

Business Plan

- If you are investing in a business in some form, a strategic plan may be needed but this depends on the investment involved. These can take many forms but it should explain how the provider or borrower plans to extract extra value from the asset with your investment.
- The plan needs to be feasible and based on reasonable assumptions and projections. You need to consider if it's a tried and tested business or asset (like property), or is this something totally new to the market and therefore unproven.
- If there has been some research undertaken (which is especially important in new markets or assets), this should be provided to support the plan.

People

- For the principal person involved in the business e.g. the developer you are investing in with, you need to review what their other business interest are at Companies House. This can be done for free.
- If this is a large investment and a wider team is involved, those key members should also be reviewed for their business interests. It also helps to understand their motivation and

experience for being involved in the business.

Fund Raising

- It's good to understand why the project is going ahead now and if this has been a smooth process, or if there have been problems in getting to this stage e.g. they've had problems with planning.

- You may want to understand more why they have approached you instead of simply obtaining bank funding (have they not been able to obtain funds from a bank?). However, this approach is now so widespread, it is not uncommon for developers to approach private investors who want a better return on their invested funds but who also have less bureaucracy.

- Establish if the funds you are being asked for achieves the borrowers fund raising target, or if there is a more open-ended expectation of the developer.

External Influences

This is sometimes referred to as a STEP (social, technical, economic and political) analysis.

- Consider the impact that any of the STEP factors may have on the opportunity. These could include changes in legislation, political leadership or governments, economic downturn and now add to the list a future virus outbreak – who would have considered that in the past!?

As you can see, there are quite a few things that you may want to review before your make an investment.

There are likely to be several types of due diligence that you may do or get carried out for you. First you could be a business owner or person who spends a few days individually investigating the financial details of a business or investment. This could then move on to where you enlist your legal and financial advisors (accountant, solicitor) to undertake an assessment. If it's a very large transaction, you will likely employ a specialised firm to perform an independent financial due diligence process on your behalf where a detailed report is then produced, the cost of which can vary widely depending on the work involved.

If you are investing with a property developer, possibly through a Special Purpose Vehicle (SPV – more on this in Chapter 8) which in itself is a company, an investor needs to be assured and understand what risks, if any, exist in the company. It is also very important to determine the value drivers (property refurbishment or planning gain for example) for the financial performance to be achieved and to be assured that the future valuations or earnings of the business are reasonable.

When done properly, a due diligence review provides valuable information to support the proposed acquisition. There is no doubt that performing an expert due diligence review could save the cost of a bad acquisition. Due diligence generally has the following objectives:

- Getting a good understanding of the historic financial situation of a company and/or the developer borrowing the money and the correctness of the reported numbers.
- Ensures that there are no hidden financial 'skeletons in the closet' which could result in future financial risks.
- Forecast of the assets future financial worth to ensure a realistic valuation and a justification of the investment or purchase price.
- The assessment could be used as a basis for further price negotiations e.g. asking for a better return on the investment due to higher perceived risks.
- Helps identify at an early stage if any information comes to light which could be a deal breaker and equally allows you to address them at this stage to see if they can be resolved.
- Obtaining a report from the due diligence process could aid bank financing.

Steps of Due Diligence and When to Start

Given that due diligence can be a costly and time-consuming exercise depending on the number of specialists involved, it is important to determine when the process should start. If you are investing in a business, you can get a better idea of when the due diligence is normally conducted as it's been done so many times, and there is a similar process that you can follow. In general, due diligence happens after the negotiations have been initially completed (and possibly a letter of intent – LOI, has been provided and signed). As a buyer, it is really useful if you can find out if, and how many, others have performed some kind of due diligence on whatever the investment is. If there are quite a few, you run a risk that you will not end up as the final buyer and will have wasted your time and money during the process. Therefore, it's worth trying to get some kind of exclusivity to the deal for at least some period of time.

Now you won't probably go to such lengths if you are simply buying a building although following a similar process may be worth considering. Once a LOI or similar agreement has been drafted that describes the structure of the deal, financial due diligence should begin. The financial due diligence process should be given enough time and money, as the analysis outcome will provide useful information about a fair purchase price. It can also help put sufficient protections and regulations in place.

The deliverables for a due diligence project can differ enormously. In general, it is good to have a report prepared if you are considering a substantial investment or purchase but only you can decide what level this is. Here are some of the contents of a standard due diligence report:

- Key findings in the executive summary.
- Details and possible risks of the financial business drivers.
- The resale values of comparable properties in similar sectors.
- Analysis of the business cash-flows.
- Financial situation analysis.
- Summary of the last calendar year(s) expenditures and review of forecasted expenses.

- Check financial or value growth forecasts and give an opinion on the achievability of those forecasts.

Having explained why due diligence is important, you can't eliminate every risk, but carrying out an appropriate amount of due diligence should greatly reduce the risks around any investment.

So, having the funds now in your SSAS account is all fine and dandy, but you won't make the fund grow without investment. Leaving the funds to wither in a bank account with little or no interest will mean it is actually losing money due to inflation.

Time to invest....

Chapter 4

Commercial Property

Owning your own residential home is a great feeling but I had always had a desire to own a commercial property. For me personally, it would take owning property to a whole new level.

There are many advantages to using a SSAS to purchase commercial property, but you must always remember that the prime purpose of buying commercial property is to provide for your future financial needs in retirement. You should be making any investment with this in mind. I remember watching an episode of 'Homes under the Hammer' and seeing a guy buy a property at auction that he paid way too much for just because he let his ego get in the way - he just had to win the auction. Following the purchase and the subsequent refurbishment works were undertaken, the revaluation showed he had made a major loss…but he "liked the building" and had brought the building "back to life." All very noble but this is not why you invest in or buy property…not for me anyway and it shouldn't be for you if your retirement is dependent on it.

So, where do we start?

Find a Property

Rightmove is a great place to start to look for commercial property but it's obviously not the only place as you can use other portals and specialist agents. A commercial agent will also be able to give you advice. However, if possible, it's always best to try and find a good time to buy a commercial property – both for you and possibly when the market is down if you can. Ideally you don't want to do it at the top of the market when prices are high and with likely downward pressures this year because of Covid-19, now could potentially be a great time to buy, but only if you have the financial means. Nonetheless, look at the trends in the local and national commercial property market. These trends include such things as:

- General values of commercial property.
- The amount of available commercial property.
- The availability of commercial mortgages (these are under pressure at the time of writing due to the financial crash caused by Covid-19).
- The quantity of competing investors.
- Finally, the likely tenant demand and rental values – obviously important if you plan to let out the commercial property, which is clearly an option.

The location and building type are also key factors when it comes to deciding which commercial property to buy. The 4 major considerations when thinking about the type of commercial building to purchase include:

1. Type of property (retail, offices, leisure or industrial).
2. Type of investment (freehold or leasehold and personally I would always go for freehold so you have the control).
3. Size (think about your likely tenant if you plan to rent the building out).
4. Location (again, think about the tenant you will be targeting or your own if you plan to use it for your own business).

In addition to the above points, you should think about how the property will suit yours or your tenant's business needs and consider at least the following points:

- Transport links – be these for haulage or for staff and include air, sea, rail and road.
- Parking facilities and restrictions – again for both haulage, delivery and staff requirements.
- Local facilities for staff like cafes, bars, open spaces.
- Position or closeness to other businesses (if this is important) like suppliers or customers.
- Building layout – will it allow for building development or expansion if needed.

One particular type of commercial property you might want to investigate buying (if you are interested in using it for your own business) is a shop in a location where there is an active Business Improvement District (BID). This is an enterprise-led collaboration offering additional resources to local businesses. Another option may be to locate a business unit in an Enterprise Zone. Zone-based companies will benefit from a variety of incentives, including a business rate discount of up to 100 percent and streamlined local authority planning. Having said that, retail shops have had a torrid time and who knows where this part of the market will end up.

Types of Property to Invest In

A lot depends on your budget and the type and amount of space you require.

If you intend to use it for your own purposes, you should think about developments in the wider commercial sector and how they could affect the type of property you would need. Conversely, if you're planning to let the building, you'll want to know what sort of premises would be in demand now and in the future e.g. a trade counter.

Click-and-collect DIY services exploded during the recent crisis as no one was allowed to make contact with each other. Wickes was one retailer that had a click-and-collect service in addition to its normal store service, but it rapidly had to establish an increase in availability of the collection service so it could keep operating. Those stores that were already set up for these types of purchases (like Screwfix) still managed to keep operating throughout the lockdown (I know as I was a frequent visitor to their stores during the completion of several building projects I had on the go at the time).

If you plan to invest in such buildings, you will need to consider how such trends might affect your business (if you plan to be an owner occupier) or your tenant's. Obviously depending on the type of building you invest in will determine the needs for you or the tenants who lease the property. If they are a retail tenant, will they need to lease a property with space suitable for collection points?

All commercial buildings are not the same and there are a number of different types that are formally categorised into different classes.

Commercial property is divided into classes of use under the 1987 Town and Country Planning (Classes of Use) Order. The legislation sets out the type of occupation for each commercial property that is possible. It is necessary to ensure that any business conducted in the commercial property is in accordance with its use in planning

The following list gives an indication of the use classes:

- A1 shops.
- A2 financial and professional services.
- A3 restaurants and cafés.
- A4 drinking establishments.
- A5 hot food takeaways.
- B1 business.
- B2 general industrial.
- B8 storage or distribution.
- C1 hotels.
- C2 residential institutions.
- C2A secure residential institutions.
- C3 dwelling houses.
- C4 houses of multiple occupation.
- D1 non-residential institutions.
- D2 entertainment and leisure.
- Sui Generis – not really a category really but this is meant to cover items not in the above list. This would include things like petrol stations, nightclubs, theatres etc.

The above list provides a guide to the use classes order in England and once again I don't suggest this list is absolutely comprehensive (there are also sub-categories to some of these classes). The classes can also be subject to interpretation and amendment. If you plan to redevelop a building or alter its intended use, you are likely to require planning permission (unless the change can be carried out under permitted development rights). It is important that you always seek professional advice from the local council, a commercial estate agent or other relevant professional on the feasibility of such changes, and ideally before you buy a property.

Holding Property in your SSAS

There are a number of key advantages from holding property within your SSAS pension. The following is a simple list of what these advantages are:

- You can elect to invest up to 100% of your SSAS pension fund into commercial property land and/or a part property purchase.
- Any gain on the property value is free from capital gains tax – this is without doubt the best reason to hold property in your pension.
- The rent is paid directly to the pension scheme's bank account and this again is free of any tax (after receipt) on the funds received and are not deemed to be contributions – meaning each member is still able to contribute up to their personal annual allowances.
- Approved assets held within a pension scheme are outside the member's personal estate for inheritance tax calculations.
- There is an opportunity to borrow funds towards or after the purchase and these could be used to subsequently develop the property, by using a commercial mortgage for example.
- It's usually not accessible to creditors in the event of your personal or business bankruptcy.
- A property can be purchased in conjunction with other SSAS members, such as work colleagues or family members.
- There is no individual or corporate liability on SSAS loans.
- On the SSAS holder's death, the property can be transferred to a beneficiary effectively as a 'death benefit'.
- The SSAS can borrow up to 50% of its value to acquire a

commercial property.

Financing a Property Purchase

There are several ways to finance your commercial property transaction. These can include borrowing (via a mortgage), a joint venture (JV) with other parties (other SSAS pension schemes for example) and via contributions to your pension scheme which could include transfers from your other pension schemes (called in specie transfers).

Borrowing - your pension scheme can borrow to help with the acquisition of investments, for example through a commercial mortgage, to aid the purchase of a commercial property. The maximum level of borrowing allowed is 50% of the net asset value of the pension scheme. These borrowings would usually come from a bank, at a rate as favourable as possible to the SSAS. A bank's borrowings are usually secured on the SSAS-owned property and demand capital and/or interest payments are funded by the rental income the SSAS receives. Any current borrowing must be accounted for under the 50% fund cap and borrowing cannot be extended to meet VAT. It is also permissible to borrow from a connected party if it can be proved that a third party lender would have secured borrowing on identical terms.

Joint Venture - a further way to fund a property purchase can be by doing this jointly with several other SSAS's, as well as with yourself (privately), your company or another third party – effectively a JV. This is also known as a joint property arrangement. There is no need to have an existing business partnership for this to be possible. You will need to establish from the beginning what each party/SSAS's share of the property will be. This will naturally reflect the amount of funds each member contributes to the gross purchase price.

There will need to be some kind of written agreement established where each enters into an arrangement to establish that the property is held on trust. The agreement will set out what proportions are owned by each member of the property and will also cover things such as the death of one of the parties, retirement or the sale of any member's share. In each of these situations a revaluation of the property would be needed. A separate bank account will need to be established for the property, and this will receive the rental payments, pay any borrowings e.g. mortgage, and hold any surplus funds until or if the trustees want to distribute the funds to each scheme/member. Any distribution will also be proportionate to each party's share.

In Specie Transfer - You can transfer a property from one of your other pension holdings to your SSAS. This is known as an in specie transfer and is the transfer of the legal ownership of an acceptable property held in another of your pension schemes to the trustees of your SSAS pension scheme as part of the transfer of your accrued benefits. Such a transfer is not normally subject to Stamp Duty Land Tax, Land and Buildings Transaction Tax (for properties in Scotland) or VAT (where the property has been opted to tax) provided the transfer qualifies as a Transfer of a Going Concern. It is worth noting that at the time of writing, there had recently been a legal challenge by HMRC around some of these taxes used specifically by SIPP providers as HMRC felt these were not being used correctly. The effect of the ruling is that individual tax relief granted on all in specie contributions must be paid back to HMRC. The legal understanding around this is ongoing so it would be worth checking with your legal and financial representatives what the latest understanding for this is and how it may affect SSAS pensions.

Some other key points of commercial property investment in your SSAS are as follows:

- It is possible for one pension scheme to buy part, or all, of another's share of the property. Unequal borrowing for joint property purchases is permitted.

- The SSAS can register for VAT where the property is (or is to be) subject to VAT. This allows the SSAS to reclaim the VAT paid on the purchase and/or development of the property.

- Finally, the SSAS can lease the property to an unconnected third party as well as to your business or some other connected party. If the lease is to a connected party the rent must be the open market rent set by a chartered surveyor and the other lease terms must be standard.

Commercial Property Risks

Probably the biggest risk with a commercial property is that it's generally an illiquid asset, which means it could take months or years to sell at the right price if for some reason you decide you need to sell it. Like all property should potentially be viewed, investment in commercial property is a long term one. Unlike a residential property where there are lots of people out there that will buy a property because it's a known asset, if a commercial property is for sale (especially if it's in a poor state or has other issues) then the pool of people that may be interested in it is much, much smaller.

When buying a commercial property, it is always worth having a plan B.

What I mean by this is that although you may be buying it for your own business use or perhaps for rental to commercial tenants, but if that strategy does not work, could it be converted to residential use? If it's a large warehouse type property, could it be easily sub-divided so that smaller business tenants could occupy the building? If you have a plan B, it will be much easier to weather difficult financial times.

Other things to consider are the following:

- The SSAS administrator is obliged to chase rent, even if it's your own business.
- Regular revaluations may be required which incur cost (think a £1,000+ rather than £100's for a residential property).
- SSAS loans (such as a loanback) tend to be short term, which can make them expensive, but will likely be cheaper than external bridging to aid a property purchase (I personally believe it is actually better to think of a loanback like bridging finance, but it's your own SSAS that is providing the finance).

So, as you would expect with any financial investment, there are risk elements you need to consider but that said, investing in property, if done correctly, is still potentially a wise thing to do. Having outlined how you consider buying commercial property, here are a few case studies on actually buying commercial property.

Case Study 1 - Commercial Multiple Occupancy (CMO)

This is the most fundamental use of having a SSAS and I am going to use an example of a commercial property that I actually purchased. This property was bought at auction at the height when Covid-19 was ravaging the world. The UK was not yet in lockdown but the death toll was starting to rise rather alarmingly in countries like Italy. There was a lot of fear around quite naturally and the stock market had plummeted.

Now one of my favourite sayings that is accredited to Warren Buffet is "Be fearful when others are greedy, but greedy when others are fearful." Pre Covid-19, I had convinced myself 2020 was going to be a good year for growth and had decided I was definitely going to "be greedy" in growing my portfolio.

I had found a commercial property on Rightmove by pure chance that was set up as an office for multiple tenants. One morning after I had finished a 4 hour writing session for this book (I used to get up at 4am to write undisturbed for 4 hours several times per week – this was my method and it worked for me), I happened to go onto Rightmove to see what commercial properties were in an area close to my home within 40 miles. Right at the top was a commercial office property not 5 minutes' drive from my home to be sold at auction, and I knew it well as it was quite close to one of the pubs in a local village. The guide price was shown as £300,000 which I was amazed at it being so low (but clearly a tactic to entice people to attend the auction), especially with the rental income being stated as £38,000 per annum.

Having not bought at an auction before, I spoke with some more experienced commercial investors in my network to get their thoughts. They agreed it was a good investment but felt the price was set to entice people to attend the auction (which is a well-known auction trick) and that they expected it to sell way above the guide price. Ok but even if this sold at £440,000 it would deliver over an 8% return which is above the stock market average – certainly my average anyway. I decided that would be my maximum bid at auction.

My unallocated funds in my SSAS pension would not cover this figure so I would need to raise some funding. I spoke with a commercial mortgage broker who advised me that getting a commercial mortgage completed within 30 days could be done but it would limit my providers and I would "...pay through the nose..." for such a quick turnaround. Hmmm...I needed to fund this another way. I then discussed this opportunity with my SSAS pension administrators who advised me that it would be perfectly acceptable for me personally to lend my SSAS the funds to complete the auction purchase and then arrange a commercial mortgage post auction. The only problem was I did not have nearly £200,000 in liquid assets available...but fortunately I knew someone that did. An investor that I had done a deal with previously and that I had just returned all of his money back to for a good return was looking for his next investment. I offered him an 8% annual return for lending me the funds for 3-6 months pro-rata while I got the mortgage sorted out. He agreed to lend me the money with just a personal guarantee. So, I now had the funding in place.

Next the legal elements. I had received the legal pack and a lot of other good information from the auctioneers. I sent this to my solicitor who cast his eye over it for no charge. There were 6 sitting commercial tenants in the building, all on 3-year leases with no right to renew their lease and there had been a rent review only a few months earlier establishing the rental incomes. The building was freehold and not subject to VAT. The information had an asbestos report and various other pieces of really useful information. The solicitor said it all looked good and this was all giving me confidence that this was potentially a good purchase.

The auctioneer arranged an open viewing date which was very well attended by around 20 people, some of them turning up in very fancy cars. This was a good and bad sign. The good sign was that a lot of people thought it was worth inspecting and therefore a good purchase, the bad sign being there would be a lot of interest and therefore competition at the auction.

Just after the viewing, the situation with Covid-19 was getting worse with more and more restrictions on people's movement. The pubs and restaurants were forced to close and there was more fear generally around about the impact the virus was having but the auction was still planned to go ahead. Within a few days the auction company advised that due to government guidelines and limits on the size of gatherings, no attendance would be allowed and the auction would be by telephone bid only. So, I then had to complete various forms to be allowed to bid which included proof of funds (for the deposit), proof of residency, proof of identification etc. Interestingly the telephone bid form included a proxy bid or max bid level. This basically meant I had to state what my maximum bid would be "in case the telephone line went down during the auction." This made me very nervous and after consulting with my network again, I decided against stating my max bid on the form and I informed the auction company that if I did not win due to such a circumstance, it was obviously not to be.

Come the day and time of the auction there was supposed to be a live feed of the auction as it happened. I was sent the link but this took me to a YouTube live feed which simply stated that there would be no live feed due to Covid-19 – WTF!! I had already been informed that I would be called when the Lot I was interested in was about to be sold but all the above elements had made me uneasy (and others as I was about to find out) but I decided to press ahead. So I was called and I could hear the auctioneer in the background preparing for the sale and then the auction started, I had already decided not to bid until people started to lose interest. The bidding started at £250,000 and rose in £5,000 increments until it reached £300,000 and then stopped. "Do you want to bid?" I was asked by Sean, the auction representative on the line'. "No" I said and waited. The price then started to move again with a new bidder coming in at £305,000. It then continued up to £315,000 and stopped again and I still had not bid. "Do you want to bid?" I was asked again by Sean......I waited and I could hear the auctioneer say "It's going once...", "Sean bid £320,000" ...I had joined the bidding as a new bidder and it seemed there was only one other person interested. The price increased to £330,000 but the other bidder was slowing down with his responses and we then started to increase in £1,000 increments. The bidding reached £339,000 in the other bidder's favour and I then bid £340,000 and there was no response from the other bidder. There was a long pause and I thought I had secured the property. The auctioneer said "I'm selling for the second time" and then came the bid of £341,000 from the other bidder – bastard! Anyway, I thought briefly and felt the other bidder was really at his maximum but I decided the next bid would be my last. "Sean, bid £342,000" which he did and there again was no response from the other bidder. "I think you've got this Richard" said Sean…" selling for the last time" I could hear the auctioneer say…" Sold!"

Somehow, I had just secured my first auction purchase.

Let's look at the numbers for this purchase:

Purchase price	£342,000
Rental Income	£38,000
Gross Yield	11%

As the property was purchased for only £342,000, I would be using most of my available SSAS funds to complete the purchase plus additional fees, with around £120,000 being borrowed from my personal funds (for which I charged my SSAS commercial rates of interest) until the commercial mortgage is arranged to cover the difference.

Just as an additional note, some may say that doing such a deal at a time when people were losing their lives to the virus and the country was focussed on the effects of Covid-19 was incredibly insensitive. My response to this would be that different people deal with situations in very different ways. For me, my way of dealing with everything that was happening with the crisis in the UK was to remain calm and to continue to focus on my property business. One of my daughters works in the NHS as a midwife, so I was acutely aware of what was actually happening in hospitals at that time. That said, as I was not a doctor or medically qualified, there was little I could do apart from 'stay home' like everyone was told at the time. I am already a volunteer for a number of organisations (one being a medical institution) and have been for a number of years, and this I will continue to do long into the future.

A final side note, if you are used to managing your own property portfolio, you can do the same with your commercial property held in your SSAS if you want to. In order to determine the correct amount you can charge, you will need to obtain quotes from 3 local property management companies, you take the average fee of these and this is what you can charge the pension scheme for your services.

Now here is another case study from a couple who have run a business for many years and as well as buying a commercial property, it helped improve their inheritance tax liability.

Case Study 2 – Commercial Building for Owner Occupation

June and Terry Phillips had been running their recycling limited company business successfully for many years, and the business had grown over this time. As their business grew year by year, they had added more employed staff and as they currently rented their business premises, they wanted to expand but have more ownership of where the business operated from.

June had been looking for a suitable property for around 18 months and found one that was fairly close to where they currently operated from and which was on the market for just over £400,000 but they negotiated this down to £387,000. Finding a premises close to their current location was important as they wanted to retain as many of their current team as possible. The more difficult task was deciding how to fund the purchase of the building.

Their business had always been profitable and their operating overheads were relatively low as they did not have a lot of capital expenditure. Historically this had enabled June and Terry to enjoy the benefits of all their hard work by extracting reasonable profits from the business in the form of annual dividends. The success of the business had also meant that the company had some decent cash reserves.

They could have almost purchased the new building themselves outright had they wanted to do so. However, they were becoming more and more conscious that their continued success was creating a potential inheritance tax (IHT) problem. With several children and grandchildren between them (some of them also working in the business), they sought advice from their accountant and their financial advisor.

Considering the Options

Working with both their accountant and IFA (Independent Financial Advisor), they discussed various options for the building purchase. The options were i) their company purchases the building, ii) they buy the building in their personal names, iii) they purchase it through a pension wrapper like a SSAS. Working with their advisors, June and Terry gained an understanding of the pros and cons for each of the above options.

June said "We were really conscious of the fact that some of our adult children were already members of the business and we really liked the idea of being able to pass the property down to the next generation with no IHT implications."

"Another key consideration for us all was the extraction of cash from the business. We realised that once funds were paid into our personal bank accounts, the dividend payments became part of our personal wealth for IHT calculations and we had already established enough wealth between us to be getting very close to the nil rate band level. So, the idea of accumulating additional wealth outside of our estate through a registered pension scheme was very attractive to us, particularly considering that member and employer contributions were very tax efficient in themselves."

"We'd never really given a great deal of thought to a pension scheme as we had been so focussed on the business, therefore we had not funded our existing pension scheme as much as we could have in the past."

Between them, they had accumulated funds of £280,000 in their existing pension, mostly from the capital growth of a single really high performing tech share in their SIPP. They also wanted to keep their salaries low as part of wider tax planning and so accepted that the scope for them to make larger contributions was limited because of their focus on dividends.

Using a SSAS

Having weighed-up all factors, and having taken the advice given by the specialist advisors, June and Terry agreed to transfer the funds in their existing pension scheme (which happened to be a SIPP that was investing in the stock market generally) into a SSAS. It became very clear that using a SSAS simply widened-out the investment powers available to the trustees (which would be June and Terry supported by an external SSAS administration company) and enabled the direct purchase of the commercial property they wanted. They had also discussed pension plans with some of the family in the business, and they could see that having a SSAS would also allow them the flexibility to add members at a later date.

As they already had an established business with many years of business accounts, this meant that setting up a SSAS would be fairly straight forward and they could then transfer their existing pension fund to the SSAS that would be created.

With the establishment of the SSAS (at the time this took around 4 months to complete, although HMRC seem to be much quicker now at establishing a SSAS pension) and the transfer of the funds from their SIPP, June and Terry arranged for their limited company to make an employer contribution of £120,000 into the SSAS (using some unused annual allowance) giving them a total fund of £400,000. They were even more pleased when they were made aware that this contribution would be treated as a business expense through the company's profit and loss account (P&L) and therefore greatly reduce its corporation tax liability, without it adding to their personal wealth for IHT purposes.

As trustees of the SSAS, June and Terry purchased the industrial building with the cash held within the SSAS bank account. The property was then immediately leased to their limited company at a commercial rate (they used a RICS registered valuer's figure to ensure the fee was seen as a semi-independent valuation) and this confirmed an annual rent of £38,995 which they were comfortable with as this was effectively being paid to them within their pension pot.

Looking at the numbers:

Purchase price	£387,000
Rental Income	£38,995
Gross Yield	10%

How did they feel about this rate of return?

"This was a great rate of return and it's worth remembering that this is money from the business that is now being used to increase our pension holding – it's like paying yourself twice because of the tax benefits!"

June and Terry were able to realise a number of benefits from this whole process.

Firstly, the rent from their business was being received tax free into the SSAS to grow for their retirements and future generations. Secondly, it was a further business expense through their company's P&L account, thereby reducing their profit and thus their tax bill. Thirdly, and very importantly for them, the £38,995 annual rent was not inflating the value of their personal wealth as it would have done if they had personally bought the property and leased it to their business.

For June and Terry, the real benefit nonetheless came in the fact that the property was growing in value, free of the main taxes (income tax, capital gains tax and inheritance tax) and that the property through the SSAS could be passed on down through the generations free of IHT.

"Having something that we knew we could pass on to our children and grandchildren without all the tax complications that normally come with inheritance was just amazing."

Chapter 5
Share or Trust Purchase

Although the investment opportunities of property and some other financial products within a SSAS are attractive and have been detailed in previous chapters, this type of pension scheme enjoys a considerable number of options for financial investment opportunities. These include:

- Hedge funds - an alternative pooled investment that is designed to protect investment portfolios from market uncertainty, created by banks and insurance companies.

- Corporate bonds – offered by companies that generally yield somewhat better returns than gilts, these are fixed-interest securities.

- Gold – subject to certain conditions, members can invest in gold bullion (not coins).

- Government gilts – offering fixed interest returns and securities.

- Deposit accounts - a SSAS pension can place its funds into an account with an accredited financial institution.

- NS&I – income bonds.

If you think you are predominantly going to invest in this kind of financial product, then potentially you are more likely to do this via a SIPP (especially as it's a cheaper product), but you clearly have the choice. You can obviously invest in these areas with a SSAS but I would see most of these kinds of investments for the 'dregs' of money you have not directly invested in other non-financial assets (or your business) in some form. Having a SSAS where the bulk of your portfolio is invested in the financial markets in some form doesn't make the most of the opportunities available with a SSAS or cheaper pension options.

The only one I'll exclude from the above statement is for NS&I income bonds. This is because you may have funds that you are planning to use with an investor, or other such investment. You are going to want to be able to access these funds quickly, without worrying about the financial consequences of accessing the funds. Putting them in an NS&I income bond account is a great way to have the funds separated from your main SSAS bank account for security purposes (in the event of a financial crash) and the speed of access cannot be faulted. As an investor, you might say you need the funds next week - no problem. You simply send a letter to NS&I signed by the trustees, request the funds to be paid into a nominated bank account and they are there within a week.

Why would you want to buy shares using your SSAS pension?

Well often it is not possible to use up all of your available pension funds in property investment or purchases and you could be left with some 'dregs' which are earning little interest. These amounts could be £1,000's or £10,000's depending on where you are with your investment process. You could be looking to diversify your investment portfolio away from being exclusively property. It is often the case that property investors/developers are highly weighted towards property investment which is exactly what this book is about, but it is worthwhile considering other options for at least some of your funds, and stocks & shares allow you to do this. Additionally, property is not 'liquid' and so accessing funds if urgently needed is not a quick process, taking anything between 3-6 months to sell a property asset. Shares on the other hand can be sold in a day with funds being available within less than 24 hours if so wished.

The trustees can invest up to 5% of the net asset value of the SSAS in shares of a sponsoring company if they wish, but it appears there is no limit for investing in companies (even unlisted ones) that are not sponsoring companies even if they are connected.

Now even though I have just mentioned buying shares in unlisted companies, for the rest of this chapter I am only going to discuss listed shares (these are shares available on the stock market). Unlisted share purchases are not something I want to go into detail here except to say buying unlisted shares as part of a SSAS investment needs very careful handling and consideration, and a clear exit strategy when you need to get your money out if needed or desired. If you want to know more on this subject, speak to your specialist advisor.

Back to buying shares in the stock market, which is an extremely easy process these days when buying shares in your personal name. There are many varied ways you can do this including buying them online through your own bank's portal. If you buy them through your bank account you will have already established your proof of identity and residency in the UK, along with having ready access to the funds you want to use to buy shares.

When you want to buy shares in your SSAS pension's name there are a few more hurdles to navigate but again these are mostly straight forward. It is likely the broking house, if you choose to use such a firm for your share purchases, will want the following documentation in order to set up a trading account in your SSAS pension's name:

1. SSAS pension dealing account application form completed by all members/trustees.

2. SSAS bank account details – this is to both receive funds from and to make payment when shares transactions are made.

3. Latest certified copy of the trust deed and rules for the SSAS pension scheme.

4. Latest certified copy of the bank statement of the SSAS pension scheme.

5. HMRC confirmation of the SSAS pension scheme tax reference number (PSTR) certified letter.

6. Obtaining a Legal Entity Identifier (LEI) number or evidence one has been applied for.

LEI's are now required for all companies (remember, I said your pension is like running a company) that wish to trade on the financial markets in the UK or within the European Union[8]. These changes occurred on

3rd January 2018 when the Markets in Financial Instruments Directive and Regulation took effect.

Whilst individuals are not affected by these changes, entities such as trusts, companies, pension funds, charities, academy schools, partnerships, and some unincorporated societies may be. LEI's are designed to identify the legal entity that is entering into financial transactions, not the financial instrument, so the process for applying for a LEI is the same for all legal entities, regardless of what instrument they will be trading.

The broking house you join for trading will likely have a process that means they can apply for a LEI on your behalf. Alternatively, there are online portals you can use to apply for the LEI and these are likely to be cheaper than going through your broking company.

Each LEI number that is issued to a pension is only active for a period of 1 year. After each year, the LEI needs to be renewed for the following 12-month period. You should renew your LEI in a timely manner so that your trading is uninterrupted. If you do allow your LEI to lapse, it is no longer active and therefore it is not possible to use it for financial trading. In cases where you know in advance that you require your LEI to be active for a longer period of time, you can renew your LEI 2 months before the renewal date.

If you have a SSAS pension administration company supporting you as a trustee (and it's probable you will), it is most likely they will be able to supply certified copies of the documents required by the broking house. Failing that, you'll need to get your own certified copies and these can be supplied by your accountant providing they have a recognised professional qualification (which they obviously should).

Once you've gone through this process you are now ready to trade using a small percentage of your pension funds if you so wish.

Reasons to both Purchase and Avoid Share Investment

As previously stated, and as I will continue to remind you through this book, I am not in a position to give you financial advice, and I certainly wouldn't advise you whether you should or should not invest in shares.

It will and must be a decision for the trustees of the pension to make and there are many advantages and disadvantages to trading in shares.

Share investment offers plenty of opportunities:

- It can take advantage of a growing economy or even the boom and bust cycle - as the economy grows, so do business revenues. Economic growth creates jobs because it creates sales and thus income. If people feel wealthier, they tend to spend creating consumer demand, which drives even more revenues into companies' cash registers.

- It can be a great way to stay ahead of inflation - historically, stocks have provided an averaged return better than inflation. This means that you can hold if there is a slight downtown in you stocks value.

- Easy to buy – with so many businesses online now, it's even possible to buy shares online making it easy to buy shares of companies. You can of course buy them the traditional route through a broker. Once you've established an account, you can buy stocks in minutes. Some online brokers allow you buy and sell stocks commission-free by way of a subscription service to their platform.

- It's possible to make money in two ways – dividends and share price growth. Most investors buy with the aim of buying a share at a low price and then to sell it at a higher price and make a profit, with a very short term or longer-term time horizon. The first group hopes to take advantage of short-term trends, while the latter expect to see the company's earnings and stock price grow over time. Other investors prefer a regular stream of cash. They purchase stocks of companies that pay good dividends each quarter. These companies will probably grow at a more moderate rate but the price of the shares will be more stable.

- They are very easy to sell - the stock market allows you to sell your stock at any time while it's trading. As I've stated a few times, property is generally considered 'illiquid'.

Stocks and shares are considered the opposite to property i.e. 'liquid', meaning you can turn your shares into cash quickly and with low transaction costs. That's important if you suddenly need your money in a hurry, but since share prices are volatile, you run the risk of being forced to take a loss if the market is down.

Share investment also offers plenty of hazards:

- Risk - you could lose your entire investment (this happened to me with a commodity exploration company I personally invested in on the AIMS market many years ago. The upside could have been huge, but they went bust instead. If a company is doing poorly or some catastrophe befalls it (think BP and that oil spill or the VW emissions scandal), investors will sell sending the stock price over a cliff edge faster than lemmings.

- Small shareholders get paid last – preferred stockholders and bondholders/creditors are first in the queue to get paid first if a company is wound up. To reduce your risk exposure, you are wise to consider a sufficiently diversified portfolio of stocks to invest in.

- Research time involved - if you are buying stocks based on your own research and efforts, it will take a lot of time to do this effectively. You'll need to read financial statements and annual reports (just like Warren Buffett does) and follow the company's performance in the financial news. You will need to keep track of the stock market itself, since even the best company's price will fall in a market downturn or crash (such as we're experiencing with Covid-19).

- Emotions - share prices rise and fall constantly with people trying to buy low out of greed, and sell high. Try not to look constantly at the market's movements (except perhaps in more volatile times) and put 'stop-loss' orders in place to avoid losing your shirt. A stop-loss order is essentially an automatic trade order given by an investor to their brokerage. The trade executes once the price of the stock in question falls to a specified stop price to avoid excessive losses.

Please remember this is your pension, whilst I may have referred to the small amounts you may have left in your SSAS pension pot after other investments as dregs, in reality, it is still probably money you worked damn hard for over your lifetime.

At the time of writing this book, the effects of Covid-19 have had a devastating effect on the world economy with the London FTSE 100 falling by nearly 25% in quarter 1 of 2020. Being in stocks just prior to this time would not have been good. But with this crash, there are obviously opportunities to make money as the crisis diminishes and things start to improve.

I was watching the stock market quite closely and had flirted with investing in Brent Crude during the market decline due to Covid-19. Oil usage was at an all-time low as everyone was in their homes with lockdown and it got to the point where there was a lack of oil storage. It went down to under $22 and it looked a great time to invest as it was obvious it would bounce back once everyone got back to work[9]. But this kind of investment went against my personal beliefs – this being that fossil fuels are bad for the environment so I didn't invest (if I had, I could have at least doubled my money in a few months). It's at times like this you get to test your morals. For me it was far better to stick with my core beliefs when investing, even if I won't make as much of a return as I could have.

There are ways to reduce your investment risk by diversifying your investments:

- Investment types – a well-diversified portfolio can have more benefits and less drawbacks than the ownership of a single asset. This could mean having a mix of shares, bonds and commodities. Over time, it could be the best way to attain the highest return at the lowest risk.

- Company sizes - that includes large, mid and small

capitalisation companies. Capitalisation is the total share price multiplied by the number of shares. It's considered good practice, because they perform differently in each phase of the business cycle, to own shares in different sized businesses.

- Location – hold positions in companies in different countries, including the emerging markets. Diversification enables you to profit from growth without being vulnerable to any one stock.

- Mutual funds – depending on the fund you invest in, this enables you to literally own hundreds of shares. These are chosen by the manager of the mutual funds and distributed through a range of sectors and businesses.

Gambling versus Investing

This is a really important aspect to consider when investing in shares. If you are focused on property, you probably won't have much experience of investing in the stock market and when it comes to the stock market, there's a fine line between gambling and investing.

Sometimes it's hard to tell the two apart. You are trying to make money with both approaches but the differences between the two methods can be easily missed by the inexperienced investor, which is why I've focused on this aspect within my book.

So, what's the difference when it comes to share purchases between gambling on stocks and investing?

Long-term vs. Short-term Focus

If you are looking for consistent returns over a reasonable period, it is very much a waiting game. You should be looking for stocks that, having done your research, you hope will perform best over a number of years. As an investor, you ideally want a portfolio of these kinds of stocks and if you make this your approach, it should work in your favour over a period of time. If you have a sound strategy to reap the rewards over a number of years, any ups and downs either in the stock itself or in the overall market should not affect your strategy too much (unless you've picked the wrong strategy of course).

Gambling is looking for the quick return over an incredibly short time frame (days, maybe weeks or just a few months at most). It seeks almost immediate high returns, but often delivers completely the opposite because of unforeseen market fluctuations or company news. You may have watched the news headlines about the 'next thing/product' or businesses on the up and buy in just on this news, with little or no due diligence on what you are investing in (even if it's a household named company). With gambling you are likely to be making lots of trades (both buying and selling) to try and catch the curve and will pay more transaction fees because of this. If you are investing, you'll be aiming to keep these fees to a minimum.

Buying for Cash Flow or Capital Growth

Investing should be all about trying to generate cash flows (just like increasing rental incomes with property). That puts the focus on receiving dividends and finding companies that have a strong history of not only paying them out on a consistent basis, but ideally also of raising these payments. If a company does this and the dividend increases, the underlying stock usually becomes more valuable.

The thing about stocks is that they can provide both capital growth and a regular income stream. As an investor this means you gain from both an income source as well as long-term growth (growth based on the business growing). In this situation with the potential for even higher dividends, an investor will likely hold onto his stock even if the price drops slightly.

Gambling is basically where you are trying to game the system to get a quick growth on the price you paid. The gambler wants to get in and probably out quickly and make a very quick return. He may hold the stock if he thinks the stock will continue to rise in price but when it starts to slow or stop rising, he cashes out and starts to look for his next purchase. The issue with any type of gambling is that you can get quickly addicted to buying and selling and the roller coaster of the highs and lows. Like any addiction, it's a bad place to be.

Another thing you may be doing as a gambler is buying on trends. What this means is that you may buy based on a rising stocks upward trend (thinking it must continue), or that you are buying the latest 'hot stocks' because everyone seems to be saying it's the next best thing since sliced bread. But in reality, you are doing nothing other than betting that a trend will continue upwards for a long enough that you'll be able to make money and move on later.

Fundamentals

As an investor you should be very aware what the standing is for the company you are investing in, the competitiveness of its products and any planned new products or services under development (which will drive its future growth). It's also good to remember you are investing in a business run by people, so get to know who the key players are in the management team as they are the ones deciding the profitability of the business and therefore future share values or dividends. Investing is also concerned with valuation measures, such as price-earnings-ratio (this is the ratio for valuing a company that measures its current share price relative to its per-share earnings) and something called book value (this is the equity per share which effectively indicates a firm's net asset value (total assets - total liabilities) on a per-share basis. This is getting quite detailed now and to go further is beyond what this book is about, but it is worth understanding some of these business indicators before you invest your pension funds.

If you are gambling, you probably won't give much time to consider a business's fundamentals, being under the false belief that if a shares price is rising, the management team must be good and the fundamentals must also be right.

Diversification

As an investor, you should be concerned about the fundamentals of all the assets you invest in, be this property, shares, holding cash reserves etc. By default, you should also be diversifying your investments, of which shares could just be one element of your overall investment strategy. Investing is about building a mix of assets likely to grow over decades and thus provide a legacy that you can pass on to your beneficiaries.

If you are gambling and being focused on chasing the biggest bang for your buck, you will probably try and put all your funds in what you think is the best performing stock and reducing the diversification of your share portfolio. So, for example if oil is rising, you might put 80% of your funds just in this one area, with the other 20% maybe in one or two other sectors or businesses. Whilst this is a strategy that potentially can pay off really well in times of crisis such as when a virus rocks the stock market, it's not a good long-term strategy.

So that's a very brief run through of how to invest in the stock market. If you plan to invest quite a large sum in the stock market, you will definitely need to educate yourself beyond what I've briefly covered here. The key thing is carrying out due diligence and understanding the fundamentals on the companies or funds you plan to invest in.

Case Study 1 – Share Purchase

Here is some share dealing I actually did with some funds from my SSAS.

I was in a situation where I had my SSAS funds diversified in commercial property, had made some loans to developers via SPV's and also had a small amount in cash held in NS&I income bonds (which is accessible within a few days).

I decided that I did not need all the accessible cash in the NS&I account I had sitting there effectively dormant – not working for me due to derisory interest rates on savings. I therefore transferred some funds back to my SSAS bank account (leaving a small percentage still in the income bond account for emergencies – effectively cash) and then transferred the balance to the SSAS broker's account I had set up. This was a non-advisory service, so just like my SSAS purchases it was all down to me.

Now with the sudden decline in share prices due to the virus, I was pretty certain there was a buying opportunity and felt that there would be a fairly rapid bounce-back for some sectors of the economy. It was clear that some were going to take years to recover e.g. the airline industry, but others would likely recover more quickly as lockdown measures improved. However, I also felt there were going to be some great buying opportunities in the autumn for commercial property and here's why.

Although many businesses were being propped up by the governments furlough scheme, many economic analysts were predicting that when this scheme of government support came to a close at the end of the summer, some of these same businesses were going to the wall. In other words, the furlough scheme had only prolonged the demise of some failing businesses. This would be applicable unfortunately both to large and small businesses in all kinds of sectors. This would undoubtedly mean that there were likely to be commercial buildings coming on to the market and I wanted to be in a position to buy one or two if I could.

Going back to share purchasing, during the lockdown I'd taken the opportunity to review a number of companies and commodities to be ready to target to buy some shares in. Having initially identified some potential targets, I planned to call the broking house ready to invest......but then I stopped.

I realised I was planning to buy shares in a number of business based on the hope that I could:

- Sell the shares quickly (maybe in a few months) ready to aid the purchase of some commercial property following the autumn, or
- Sell the shares quickly if it looked like there was another dip and try and 'catch the curve' before everything goes pear shaped.

What did this mean? Well, I was effectively gambling!!

Based on the profiles we've reviewed earlier in this chapter, I was gambling (or calculating) that I could pick some shares that were priced low and I would watch them rise before selling for a profit to invest in more property. We were in "unprecedented times", in fact the use of the word 'unprecedented' was unprecedented! So, I felt that the risks for my investments were quite low provided I stayed with the fundamentals of investing long term but expected to see a fairly short-term gain. But who was I kidding – this was my pension, I shouldn't be gambling with my pension!

I reminded myself of the fundamentals of share investing which is about being patient and seeking consistent returns over the long-term. The focus should be on buying stocks that will perform best over a period of years. Equally, as well as property development, I was getting more and more interested in renewable energy, as well as the opportunities that were likely to come with the 5G explosion in products that would use the 5G networks. As a result, I decided these sectors should become part of my portfolio for my share purchases.

I'd listened to many property podcasts from people saying "If only I'd bought more property in 2009 when prices were low!"- I should know as I was one of them. I wasn't going to be found wanting again given this opportunity in the stock market.

So, I purchased a number of stocks in a variety of sectors. These included companies establishing the 5G network which some analysts were saying will see massive growth over the coming decade[10]. Also I invested in renewable energy and some tech companies that I think will benefit from the fantastic decision of the British people to fully endorse Brexit and the global trade deals that will come about as a result of this.

For share purchases, you'll pay stamp duty on your purchases. This is charged at 0.5% on share purchases made electronically (e.g. an online share dealing account). For non-electronic deals, it's charged at 0.5% on transactions valued over £1,000.[11]

Now I may have sold my shares (or maybe now plan to sell them depending on having found another commercial property opportunity) by the time you are reading this, and that sale would give me additional funds in my SSAS bank account to invest in commercial property. Even if I have now sold them, I wouldn't have waited until I had the funds in my account before searching for a suitable property, I would already be searching the market for potential properties to invest in.

Most likely my target would be something like a CMO (commercial multiple occupancy) or a mixed use building (whilst being mindful of trading concerns), so a purchase with clear permitted development rights available or perhaps a lease option purchase (where the SSAS would not complete on the purchase unless it succeeded in a planning gain) was my objective.

Now due to the timing of the book's publication, I can't say if I'd yet succeeded in my objective but maybe if you see me at a networking event or contact me on social media, I'll let you know how I got on.

Case Study 2 – NS&I Income Bonds

When I first established my own SSAS, I did not have a clear strategy on how I was going to spend all the funds. I knew buying commercial property was what I really wanted to do but I needed to find a property first. I can still remember when my professional SSAS administrator contacted me on completion of my SSAS being approved to ask "Have you identified a property to purchase yet?"

She was a bit surprised when I said "No."

It did faze me for a moment as I had not seriously looked for anything, my excuse for this being that the time taken by HMRC to approve a scheme varied greatly. I didn't want to find 'the' property only to have no funds to buy it.

So, here I was now in a position to buy a property but equally I thought finding what I was looking for may take some time. Being aware that this meant I had a lot of money sitting in a single bank account made me nervous as it left me exposed in the event of a bank failure. Now I didn't know if one was around the corner, but I knew that under the FSCS, the government only protected funds up to the amount of the first £85,000 in your account (or £170,000 if your money is held in a joint account[12]) should that bank or building society go bust – I had way more than that in the bank account set up to hold my SSAS money, so I needed to think how I could protect it and reduce such a risk?

Following a discussion with the accounting firm that had arranged the transfer of my original corporate pension pot funds into my SSAS, we agreed that it was probably best to place this into a NS&I income bond account. It would mean that the funds weren't left exposed in the SSAS bank account, but equally they were quickly accessible (liquid) to be transferred within days from the NS&I account to the bank account when needed, this assuming I would I find a commercial property to buy.

This transfer was arranged within a few days and the money was deposited safely into the income bond account.

The good thing about NS&I income bonds is that you can see the status of the account easily online. The interest you would be receiving is not going to really be worth thinking about, but in my situation it allowed for a suitable separation from the bank account and protection of the funds.

If you plan to do something similar, it's worth being aware that with an income bond account, when you want to transfer funds bank to the SSAS account to fund a purchase, you can't simply login and move money around like you can with premium bonds. Because these monies are held for a pension fund, you will need the trustees to sign a hard copy document to arrange any transfers. You complete the form (it's just one page) and nominate where you want the funds to go, send it off to NS&I and within a few days to a week the money will appear safety in the relevant bank account.

This is how I did things and whilst I did not technically put the funds in an income bond account for the returns it generated, you could obviously leave it there if you wished….but I doubt you'll think that's a good use of the money.

In the end I did find a property (you'll have read about this in the first case study in Chapter 4) and moved what I needed to allow the purchase to complete.

Chapter 6

Acceptable Residential Elements for a SSAS

Hold on, I thought you can't hold anything that has a residential element in a SSAS!?

Well that's generally true, in all circumstances a SSAS cannot directly own a residential property e.g. a family home, in its own name as that would break HMRC rules and result in some pretty eye-watering penalties. There are, however, certain situations where a SSAS can invest in a commercial property with a residential element.

There are certain circumstances where this is allowed and 2 specific types are:

- The property is occupied by an employee who is not a scheme member, or connected to a scheme member or connected to the employer, and they must be required to live there as a condition of their employment (e.g. a caretakers flat).

- It is occupied by a person who is neither a member of the pension scheme nor connected with such a member, and is used in connection with business premises held as an investment of the pension scheme (e.g. a pub with a flat above that is occupied by the pub manager).

In no circumstances is it allowable for the residential element in the above situations to be occupied by a scheme member or one of their relatives i.e. a connected person.

Another area where you need to tread carefully is in relation to having mixed commercial and residential sites or freeholds, usually referred to as mixed use. Where the job-related criteria are not going to be met as mentioned above, but you are dealing with a mixed-use site, then you need to be very careful that the SSAS only buys the leasehold of the commercial element. If the SSAS owns the freehold of the whole property (of which part of it is considered residential) then tax charges would apply, even where the leasehold of the residential part was owned by another party. A freehold interest in a property that is even only partly a residential property will still be considered as taxable.

Supported Accommodation

We will cover care homes in Chapter 10 but another method of investing in what would normally be classed as taxable property is something called supported accommodation.

This type of accommodation is similar in the support it provides to say, a care home, but is different in that it is for people that are physically mobile. They will have some kind of mental health disorder where they need constant support and/or cannot look after themselves in some way. Because they are mobile, this means that standard house accommodation facilities (and I'm thinking something like a large HMO) would be suitable for these people, unlike someone who is elderly and needs special facilities likes lifts etc.

The key thing is that they need a full-time carer who lives in the building.

To clarify the criteria, this means a home or other institution providing residential accommodation with personal care for persons in need of personal care by reason of past or present dependence on alcohol or drugs, or a past or present mental disorder. This is not easy property to establish.

You will probably need to set this up through a registered housing provider (housing association) who will become the management agent and can set the rent, liaise with the local housing authority with the aim to achieve exempt accommodation rates for the ingoing tenants based upon this being independent living/supported housing. The registered provider also commissions the care service which will be able to provide the care and support required by the individuals moving into the scheme. The care service will apply for care quality commission (CQC) registration in advance of occupancy.

This is a very simplistic overview of using your SSAS for this kind of investment but the detailed steps you need to go through to set this up go beyond the subject of this book. If this is something that appeals to you as a person, not just as an investor, you need to work with the specialists and local authorities to establish such an operation.

Residential Investment via a Third Party

Just to mention here, it is perfectly acceptable for a SSAS to lend funds to a third-party developer, or your own property development company to invest in residential property. As the SSAS will not directly own the residential property, this does not break HMRC rules for residential investment.

This is possible either through a loanback (covered in Chapter 7) or via a third-party developer loan through a special purpose vehicle (covered in Chapter 8).

Chapter 7

Business Loan or Loanback

Since many property investors own incorporated companies, another investment route is to obtain a loan from your pension fund into a limited company for a member. This investment method provides the funds to the investor's incorporated business to make residential property-related investments (if desired) that can be used for property deposits or refurbishment expenses. However, because SSAS pension loans are regulated by HMRC, it's important to note there are a number of requirements that must be adhered to:

- Interest rate – it must be at least 1% above the average base lending rates of the main high street banks.
- Term of loan – this must be no more than 5 years with the full amount needing to be completely repaid by the end of the term.
- Maximum amount of loan – this must be no more than 50% of the net SSAS assets.
- Repayment terms – these must be on a capital & interest basis at least annually, paid in equal instalments through the period of the loan (in other words, you can't pay everything you owe at the end of the period).
- Security – the loan must be secured by a first charge on a suitable asset, which could be an unencumbered residential property (which is where there is no finance or mortgage secured on the asset).

SSAS Loanback

In certain cases, loans from licenced pension schemes are prohibited by HMRC rules to the scheme member, or any person connected with them and thus would be subject to unwanted payment tax charges.

One exception to this provision is a loan from a pension scheme provided to the sponsoring employer. This is generally known as a Loanback and is where a loan is made from a SSAS. Let's look in a little more depth at the five rules or checks we've outlined above that need to be followed.

Interest Rate

The minimum interest rate that can be applied to an approved employer loan is specified by HMRC. This must not be less than 1% higher than the average clearing bank base rate for six designated high street banks rounded to the nearest 0.25%.

The 6 leading high street banks are:

- Bank of Scotland plc.
- Barclays plc.
- HSBC plc.
- Lloyds Bank plc.
- National Westminster Bank plc.
- Royal Bank of Scotland plc.

The applicable rate is published on HMRC's website, and this rate will be calculated at the reference date in accordance with HMRC's Prescribed Interest Rates for Authorised Employer Loans Regulations 2005.

Term of Loan

An authorised employer loan must be for a fixed term not exceeding five years. However, there is the opportunity that this can be rolled over once for an additional term not exceeding five years but only for specific reasons.

If a SSAS loan reaches the end of its term and is still partially outstanding then the loan may be extended. This is called a 'rollover'. What's more, provided that there is no increase to the amount of the loan, the rollover will not be treated as a new loan and therefore any existing security may continue, even if the security is less than the face value of the loan.

An example may be if a borrower (employer) has significant financial problems in making repayments when there is a remaining sum of capital or interest at the end of the loan term, the loan duration can be prolonged when the loan repayment date can be delayed or 'rolled over' for a term up to another five years from the normal repayment date. A loan can be rolled over only once, but any existing security may continue as importantly the rollover loan will not be treated as a new loan (providing nothing changes).

Amount of Loan

No more than 50 percent of the aggregate value of the scheme assets, at the point at which the loan is made, is allowed. This is taking into account any other current loans or borrowings. The value of the scheme is calculated as the total of any cash held, plus the market value of other assets immediately prior to implementing the loan.

Let's assume the SSAS wants to make a loan to the sponsoring business of £100,000. Before the loan is made, the schemes value is calculated and is £300,000, broken down as follows:

- NS&I Income Bonds - £66,000
- Cash in SSAS bank account - £54,000
- Commercial property (unencumbered) - £180,000

Total assets = £300,000

Therefore, the loan is perfectly acceptable as up to £150,000 could be loaned, if the funds are available.

Repayment Terms

Loan repayments for each complete year of the loan must be made in equal instalments of capital and interest. If the amount due to be repaid in any borrowing year is less than required, or a loan payment is missed, then under this requirement an unauthorised payment is considered to have been made resulting in fines from HMRC unless you can justify the non-payment.

Security

The loan must be secured by a first charge over an asset with a value at least equal to the value of the loan plus interest during its entire term. The asset does not need to be owned by the sponsoring business, but there can be no other charge that takes precedence over the charge to the pension scheme on that asset – including a floating charge.

Should the asset used as security be replaced for any reason during the term of the loan, the asset must have a value at least equal to the lower of:

• The market value of the asset being replaced; or

• The value of the remaining loan plus interest.

This will require that an independent market assessment by an accountant, chartered surveyor (RICS), or any suitably qualified individual is carried out to assess the value of the asset.

HMRC has explained its stance on the use of taxable property, such as residential property or chattels, where they are used as collateral for a pension scheme loan. If a regulated pension scheme acquires an interest in taxable property either directly or inadvertently, then normally the amount paid is treated as an unauthorised payment.

An unauthorised payment will be regarded by HMRC as having been made, where an authorised employer loan is secured against taxable property, in the following circumstances:

• The pension scheme's assets were used to pay costs (rather than, for example, by the sponsoring employer), when arranging security for the loan and which incurred legal or administrative fees. The amount paid will be treated as an unauthorised payment.

• If the loan recipient fails to maintain or complete payments, and the pension scheme is required to enforce its charge over the taxable property and becomes the owner of the property. In this situation an unauthorised payment equal to the value of the scheme's interest i.e. the outstanding loan balance will be required as HMRC will treat the charge acquisition as a further interest in the property.

In order to mitigate the risk of scheme members or the pension scheme being liable for unauthorised tax liabilities, or to provide the requisite liquidity to cover the programme administrator's tax liability, the following requirements should be followed when using taxable property as collateral for an SSAS loanback:

- The sponsoring employer of the scheme must pay any legal and administrative costs relating to the establishment of the pension scheme's charge over the taxable asset.

- Any loan agreements should state that the taxable property being used as security must be sold to resolve any default to ensure that the SSAS does not become the owner of the taxable property at any time.

A first charge may be placed on residential property that will satisfy HMRC requirements for security and should not result in an interest in the property being created on default. Due to the complexity of this matter you should ensure that your solicitor is fully conversant with the requirements to ensure every precaution is taken to prevent an unauthorised payment arising.

Purpose of Loanback

The purpose of the loan must be for business purposes that are authentic and not to just allow the sponsoring employer to continue to trade in the short term. A loan should not be credited to an insolvent company.

The borrower must use the borrowed money for a business purpose to benefit their trade or profession. Be aware that the borrower may be asked by HMRC to produce receipts or other evidence to demonstrate how the funds have been used.

Further Guidance

A SSAS is allowed to make loans to a sponsoring business however HMRC only consider the loans appropriate if they are for genuine investments that are wise, secure and on a commercial basis. Loans must not be made to the following parties:

- Scheme members, their relatives or connected parties.
- Any companies controlled by scheme members and/or connected persons excluding the sponsoring employer.
- Partnerships in which scheme members and/or their relatives are partners and includes LLPs.

The SSAS must ensure that the company is a going concern in order to make a loan to a sponsoring business, and the loan must be for commercial purposes. It must not be merely to keep an afflicted business afloat, or to be made to a technically insolvent sponsoring employer.

Trustees must also take all possible legal steps to enforce a loan's repayment if a sponsoring company breaches the terms of the loan agreement, ceases to operate or becomes insolvent. No preferential treatment must be given to the pension scheme business when enforcing debt collection, even if this involves putting the company into liquidation.

Here we have a few case studies where property has been used as security for a loanback.

Case Study 1 – Loanback for Business Expansion

Frank Dubois has a successful limited business operating within a commercial premises which he wants to expand. Just like many other small companies, he really didn't like the idea of going to a high street bank to borrow funds, mainly due to the bureaucracy involved. Ideally, he wanted to use an alternative source of funding and had been advised by his financial adviser that it could be possible to borrow money from his existing SSAS pension fund.

His SSAS was valued at £600,000 at the time which was diversified into a range of liquid investments (shares), as well as a sizeable amount available held in cash in the bank account and also within an income bonds account.

Frank and his wife have a 50/50 equal split of the total value of the pension scheme, with their limited company being the sponsoring business for the SSAS. They have always been very cautious with their investments and wanted to give careful consideration to what they wanted to do and how such an arrangement would work. They really wanted to understand what was involved and felt they needed to clarify their understanding of this approach before perhaps considering a further alternative funding method.

"We decided to have a meeting with our financial advisor" said Frank. "This was so we could understand the implications for us borrowing money from our SSAS as we'd never considered anything like this before. When our advisor told us of the implications of borrowing incorrectly and the tax implications of doing this, it scared the life out of me, I really wasn't convinced it was the right thing to do. But as we discussed it and Brian (the IFA) explained the process to us, and that he would guide us through the steps needed, we decided to go ahead."

Frank and his wife came to realise that the maximum amount of a loan which they could make to their business (the sponsoring employer) was 50% of the total value of all the assets of their SSAS. As we know that the value of the SSAS was £600,000, this would therefore mean that Frank and his wife could loan up to £300,000 to their business.

"This was absolutely brilliant and with the simple checks we would need to go through compared to that of bank borrowing, and the low amount of interest we would have to pay, it really was a no brainer" said Frank. "When we compared the amount of borrowing, we couldn't believe you could borrow money at such a low rate – it was almost like free money which we could inject into the business."

The 50% limit was applied at the date the money was lent and Frank was pleased to be reassured that should the value of the collective investments drop or interest rates go up, then the loan amount or interest does not need to be recalculated unless the terms of the loan changes – which he had no intention of doing.

Being able to loan the funds at a very low rate (just 1% above the base rate of 0.5%) was also a bonus to the business to keep cash flows so positive.

To make a loan to Franks sponsoring business, the funds had to be protected by a first charge on a suitable asset. As it happens, the commercial property where the business operates from had recently become unencumbered as the mortgage on it had been paid off and was valued (independently) at £345,000.

"I know lots of business are quite happy with high levels of debt" said Frank, "but my approach was always to get rid of any debt as quick as you can which is why I worked hard to pay off the mortgage on the business property as soon as I could. As it worked out, it was a good thing I did as this allowed the loanback to go ahead as the building provided the perfect security for the loan."

To remind ourselves, the loan made to a sponsoring employer must be repayable to the SSAS in equal instalments of capital and interest.

Here are the numbers...

Frank and his wife decided to borrow the full amount of £300,000 charged at fixed rate of 1.5% over a 5-year period. This meant the total amount that will need to be paid back would be £313,729 (£300,000 + the interest of £13,729 but we will round this down to £313,725). Therefore, the repayable amounts (using rounded numbers here) at the end of each year would be calculated as follows;

Year one (£300,000 + £13,279)/5 = £62,745 total repaid

Year two, they repay another £62,745 = £125,490 repaid

Year three, another £62,745 = £188,235 repaid

Year four, another £62,745 = £250,980 repaid

Year five, the final £62,745 = £313,725 total repaid

So in year five Frank and his wife had repaid the principal loan and the interest for the loan.

As a result of the above lending, the SSAS injection of funds provided the necessary financial support for the expansion of their business.

"It really allowed us to expand the business way beyond what we thought possible. It has really taken off and we are so pleased to have been able to utilise our own funds in this way. The repayments made by the business will be classed as a business expense, meaning that it will reduce our corporation tax liability, which is always nice to do for the right reasons."

Case Study 2 – Loanback for Property Portfolio Expansion

Jim Brown had been a successful property investor for a number of years, building up his property portfolio within a limited company that he had established whilst being employed full time in the corporate world.

He had had a varied career and had always contributed to occupational pension schemes through a number of employment positions, eventually spending most of his career with one main corporate employer. At the time, he knew this would give him a number of pension pots to draw benefits from when he retired, but this plan was modified with the changes brought in by George Osbourne, and he realised that he would be able to consolidate these into one scheme at some point if he wished to.

He had decided to set up a SSAS pension when his accountant explained the flexibility this type of scheme would give him for later investment planning, especially the ability to invest funds before normal retirement age.

Jim takes up the story.

"I set up my SSAS pension by transferring funds from occupational schemes I had contributed to throughout my corporate employment. I topped this up with a single contribution from a redundancy payment when I left my last job. Paying this into my pension avoided the higher rate income tax that would have been due on this compensation. The total fund value was now close to the lifetime allowance limit, so I was unable to contribute further, however I had a substantial fund available, half of which could be lent to my own company as a loanback."

He had originally been growing the funds in his own scheme, but revised this plan thanks to the pension changes brought in by George Osbourne in 2015, and decided that he would eventually transfer across his main final salary pension pot when he was able to. This would increase the overall size of his scheme total holdings. He would also transfer across all the other smaller pension pots he had built up over his varied career to his own scheme.

The thing that really attracted Jim to a SSAS scheme was the ability to use the loanback facility. He knew this would allow him to inject funds into his property business that he had been quietly growing adjacent to his corporate career. He would use these funds as deposits for residential property purchases which he would then rent out for a revenue stream to his property business. All his properties were held within his limited company name, so he was a little ahead of the curve in buying property in this way rather than in his own personal name. This has now become a landlord's main approach due to the tax changes implemented in April 2017 as they began to lose their tax relief under a rule known as Section 24[13].

"As I was getting closer to the age where I would be able to draw on the pension benefits if I wished, I had also made the decision to go full time in property. With this in mind I decided I wanted to accelerate the number of properties in my portfolio just before or at the time I became 55, and before I left full time employment with my corporate employer."

Jim's approach with his limited company property purchases had always been to get the debt (mortgage) paid down rather than just use interest only mortgages, so he had always taken out mortgages that were with a repayment of the interest and debt. Over time this meant he had several properties that had no finance secured on them i.e. they were unencumbered.

His first loanback was in 2017 which he arranged for £200,000 to be repaid over 5 years. The repayments would be £41,500 per year which included interest at a rate of 1.25% (1% above base rate). The interest would be £7,500. The legal fees and associated costs to arrange this were all paid by his limited company. The loan was secured with a first charge on one of the limited company properties that had no debt attached to it and the valuation was on commercial terms i.e. based on the rental revenue, which was significantly higher than if the valuation had simply been based on the bricks and mortar valuation.

Here are the numbers:

Year one (£200,000 + £7,500)/5 = £41,500

Year two, Jim repaid another £41,500 = £83,000

Year three, another £41,500 = £124,500

Year four, another £41,500 = £166,000

Year five, the final £41,500 = £207,500

So in year five Jim had repaid the principal loan and the interest for the loan.

As a result of this injection in cash, he purchased a repossessed property for cash which he converted to a HMO, then refinanced to release the funds for deposits on six more single lets. He subsequently rented these out and this further increased the revenue that was flowing into the limited company account. He was in year four of his repayment plan at the time of the interview and had made his repayments on time and according to the schedule.

He has since made a second loanback arrangement following the consolidation of all his pension pots into his SSAS when he became 55. This has greatly increased the funds available for this kind of facility. When not making a loanback to his limited company, the remainder of his funds have been used for providing loans (via SPV's) to developers known to him.

"Being able to use the loanback facility from my SSAS was a game changer for me. I was able to increase my limited company revenue stream significantly by growing my portfolio and also be totally in control of how the funds were invested. Now being 'full time' in property, I have complete flexibility to do what I want, when I want and have effectively replaced my corporate salary. I still chose to work but now it's completely on my terms. Since doing this, I moved to a different part of the country (from the South of the UK to the North) which has allowed me to pay off my own mortgage as well. In addition to running the property business, I now spend my spare time brewing my own beer which is a real passion for me. It doesn't get any better than that!"

Chapter 8

Property Bonds, Crowdfunding and Special Purpose Vehicle

It is very straight forward to loan a property developer funds to develop a property (which can be residential by the way) and get a return from the investment either as a fixed percentage rate of the loaned funds or as a profit share on the sale price or a mixture of the two. The key thing if it's residential in nature is that at no time can the SSAS become the owner of the property should there be a payment default of some kind. If it's a commercial property there is no issue. So when making such a loan which has a residential element (maybe it has always been a residential property but it is being enlarged to a HMO or similar), there needs to be a clear statement in the loan paperwork between the SSAS and the borrower that the property would need to be sold to resolve any financial default situation.

Property Bonds or Developer Loan Notes

Property bonds allow investors to get a better return for their money than leaving it to sit in a savings account, and the investment in property can be made without actually doing any of the hard work, either with the property development or the considerable challenges of dealing with tenants. Property bonds (which are sometimes called "loan notes") are essentially a corporate bond (certificate) issued by a property developer.

The investor will buy the bond or loan note (which is essentially just an IOU) and in return receives a certificate and usually security (this is not essential to comply with pension rules) over the property they're helping to fund. For this they will usually receive a fixed return (usually monthly or annually) from interest on the loan which is paid to the investor. At the end of the term, the investor's bond 'matures' and the original loan amount is returned back to them for another investment along with any outstanding interest.

Bonds can be paid for in cash or you can purchase them through the SSAS pension funds. Property bonds are a common route to real estate investment through a SSAS pension scheme. They provide a hands-off investment opportunity for SSAS members, enabling each member to enter into a loan agreement (collectively) with a property developer on a development project.

These type of loans provide the developer with the necessary funds to complete a project before selling it and/or returning the invested funds back to the investor, usually by refinancing (e.g. re-mortgaging) the development. Bonds usually range somewhere between one to two years, but they can be as long as five years.

Crowdfunding/Peer-to-Peer Lending

Another branch of lending in property development is Crowdfunding or Peer-to-Peer lending (P2P). This has grown significantly over the last 10 years and has been predominantly led by people looking for a better return on their money, rather than leaving it in poor interest paying savings accounts. At the same time, developers have been looking for alternative sources of investment away from the main banking sector.

Crowdfunding and P2P lending are often regarded as one and the same but they are not. They both involve investors coming together to provide financial support for something, usually a property development in our case. P2P is much more like a loan note in that you are providing a loan to a developer. Crowdfunding usually involves a part ownership in a development project and thus has equity in the building.

Both are a way of raising finance by asking a large number of people for a small amount of money. Traditionally for a developer, financing a property development involved asking a few institutions or people for large sums of money. Crowdfunding/P2P switches this idea around by asking lots of people (usually small investors) for relatively small amounts of money.

There are mainly two types of investment possible – debt and equity funding.

Debt Funding - here investors will receive all of their many back with an interest payment on top once the development is completed and sold. It may involve all of a building or part of a building to be sold before the investor receives their funds and interest payment. This is probably the most common route for small property investors to be involved in a large development project as it provides a clear exit for the return of their funds.

Equity Funding - in this method of funding, the investor retains some ownership of the property (or business) being developed. Funds are exchanged for a stake in the property and future profits from capital growth on a sale. Retaining ownership would seem acceptable for a commercial property investment from a SSAS, but is not possible if the property is say a commercial to residential conversion, and so a sale would be required in this instance.

Although these investing methods are now widely touted as possible SSAS investments, a SSAS administrator's willingness to accept this type of investment can vary. They may consider it a high-risk investment as you have no FSCS backing. There is also a risk that the funds might end up inadvertently invested in taxable property where the borrower does not fulfil HMRC requirements and this will result in tax charges for the Trustees. As a Trustee, when investing through such a method, you do need to know who the borrower is so you can check the HMRC rules are being adhered to.

If you want to proceed you can, but the professional administrator you use may want you to sign a full disclaimer confirming they cannot be responsible for any loss of capital or interest, and should HMRC deem the funds have been invested in taxable property and tax charges are applied, they will not be responsible for those charges. So be aware that investment via this route is not as straightforward as many funding platforms would lead you to believe. Speak to suitably qualified advisors before considering this type of investment.

There is an alternative method to property bonds, using something called a Special Purpose Vehicle (SPV).

Special Purpose Vehicles

There is a lot of misunderstanding surrounding SPVs with many struggling to understand what a SPV actually is – and how to use it. What's more, there is also a lot of confusion around using limited companies to buy properties and how to raise finance for limited companies.

If you're wondering why I've mentioned limited companies, you might not realise that whilst they may sound like separate topics, they are really just part and parcel of the same subject.

Some people consider a SPV to actually be a separate entity in its own right. This is where the confusion begins as a SPV is just a generic name for any entity that you choose for a particular purpose. A SPV is not a specific type of entity but instead a 'vehicle' or method that is used for a specific purpose to help you achieve your objectives. The vehicle in question here is the setting up of a limited company, partnership, LLP or any other type of entity…although a limited company format is generally used as this is the easiest to set up and has a formal structure for legal purposes.

Following George Osborne's decision back in 2015 to withdraw the ability to offset mortgage interest against rents when calculating income tax if you are a high rate taxpayer, more and more property investors have been buying their properties using limited companies. The reason for this is that if they buy into a limited company, they can offset all of the mortgage interest against rents when calculating corporation tax instead. Assuming things don't change with any future Budgets (or there's a change of government that results in even stronger attacks on the private rental market), then this is one possible way for investors to get around Osborne's stumbling block.

So, given the situation whereby you want to invest some of your SSAS funds with a third party, in this position a limited company is specifically set up with the sole purpose of owning one property for development purposes with an outside investor.

The ability to offset all the mortgage interest against rental income when calculating corporate tax is a major benefit for limited businesses, which is possibly the main reason why this method has become so popular after the tax reforms in Section 24 (which removes a landlord's right to deduct mortgage interest as a cost if a higher rate taxpayer).

Using a SPV

There are a multitude of ways in which you could use an SPV for property investing. If we consider the easiest you might decide to simply ask the borrower to set up a limited company (which is the SPV) which will own the property to be developed. The property will need to have no finance secured against it if you want to have a first charge to secure the SSAS investment.

A loan agreement will need to be drawn up between you and the borrower detailing the terms of the loan and interest rate. You can of course get this agreement created by your solicitor or you could potentially create your own, depending on the complexity of the loan and your own competency. It is best practice to consult with suitably qualified advisors in the creation of such a document, but the key thing here is to make sure it covers all the things you think could go wrong e.g. the development costs are higher than expected, the development takes much longer than you think to complete etc. It's not just a 'nice to have' as the only time this really comes to the fore is when things do go wrong, which they will, even if it's your best mate you are lending the money to. That said, both sides need to agree what they want to get out of the partnership and the best way is to structure the agreement to make sure that you both feel safe and protected within it.

You then arrange for your solicitor to secure a first charge of the property via the SPV and at the same time loan the developer the agreed funds. If you cannot secure a first charge on the property (perhaps because the developer did that to be able to buy the property in the first place), you then could take out a second charge. This obviously puts you at a disadvantage in terms of getting paid if something does go wrong so you then might want to consider things like personal guarantees. This is not unreasonable as on occasion when I've taken out a buy-to-let mortgage on one of my residential properties owned by my property business, the mortgage company have sometimes insisted on a personal guarantee from me just in case the business defaults, so it's quite normal practice.

I've agreed loans where I've been given a personal guarantee in similar situations, and have not agreed loans where the developer was unwilling to give me a personal guarantee. My thinking here being that if they are not willing to put things on the line if they default, why should I.

Your SSAS administration provider will also need to be closely involved to ensure all the correct legal steps are taken and that you are protected from any fines from HMRC for not doing things properly resulting in you ending up with a tax liability.

I would also recommend a unique SPV for each investment you make even if you are doing more loans to the same borrower or developer. This approach just makes everything clean if there should be a problem with one investment as it won't have a knock-on effect with other investments.

That should have shown you how relatively easy these are to set up, with the most effort going into the loan notes or the loan agreement between you and the developer (which solicitors love to crawl all over…but they are protecting your interests after all).

Security Trustee

It's probably worth mentioning something called a security trustee.

A Security Trustee (ST) is appointed for the benefit of a loan note's holder(s) to safeguard the interests of this person or group without them having to take ownership of the asset. The security involved may comprise of a charge over a property or other types of security.

The ST is independent of the loan note issuer and normally has the ability, if required, to take control of the issuer's underlying assets on behalf of the lenders, if the issuer was to be in default on payments that were due and payable under the loan agreement. This is great if your loan involves taxable property as this would ensure your SSAS never becomes the owner of the property in the case of a default.

A ST is usually (but not always) an independent entity which is regulated by the Financial Conduct Authority or equivalent financial services regulator. The most obvious advantage of involving a security trustee is that it protects the rights of the noteholders, so you need to decide as the lender if this is something you want in place.

Genuinely Diverse Commercial Vehicles

Another thing to be aware of for a SPV type of investment is something called Genuinely Diverse Commercial Vehicles (GDCV), and a 'vehicle' here simply means a person or company. GDCV is particularly important to understand when you are investing with a non-trading developer via a SPV as it's easy to fall foul of the rules.

First you need to be sure you are not connected either by blood or business e.g. you are not co-directors of a business. If you are, you cannot loan any funds.

Second, you need to establish if the purpose of the money being loaned is for trading purposes e.g. to refurbish and sell a property, or to refurbish and hold the property. If it's the former, there is no GDCV issue. If it's to buy, refurbish and hold the property, you must make sure that, as the lender, you cannot influence or control the borrower's ability to hold that money, and that the money is not directly connected to a piece of residential property.

Thirdly, if whoever you loan the money to is holding the property (plans to keep it to rent out), you need to determine if you are lending to an individual person or a company.

If it's an individual, there are 3 GDCV tests:

1. The borrower must have assets held directly of £1million, or hold 3 or more properties.

2. The borrower's portfolio must have no one property worth more than 40% of the total portfolio.

3. The amount being loaned must be no more than 10% of the portfolio value.

If it's a company (like a SPV):

- is it a 'close' company i.e. it has 5 or fewer directors or shareholders? If it is, you cannot loan to this company otherwise you will be fined by HMRC.

The above criteria not only apply when the pension scheme makes the initial investment, but also for the whole period that the pension scheme has that investment.

So, to be clear, if the vehicle is trading, there is no issue and you can potentially ignore GDCV. If the vehicle is buying and holding, it's unlikely a SPV will be suitable as it's unusual to have 5 directors in a SPV.

Case Study 1 – Conversion to Serviced Apartments

So, once again, I'm going to share one of my own experiences.

A very experienced developer contact of mine, Rupert Green has multiple residential properties (who also happened to mentor property investors like myself) and would occasionally invite me to visit the sites he was developing to share his experience. During one such visit and knowing how he worked with other investors, I approached him and asked if there were any up and coming projects that I could potentially invest in with him. He was always seeking out investment for projects and it just so happened he had one in the pipeline and said he would send me through the details.

Sure enough, within a few days he sent through some details about a potential project. It was a 3-storey Grade II Listed townhouse that he was going to develop into serviced apartments for resale. He had already agreed the purchase price and it was to be owned by a SPV he had set up expressly for this purpose. So, he was looking for support in purchasing the property and for development finance to progress the project.

Now here's the thing when you deal with an experienced developer. They know what an investor is looking for and what questions are likely to be asked. To address these points, Rupert had sent through to me a complete PowerPoint proposal detailing the percentage return on my investment funds that he was offering, the investment he was making into the property, what the gross development costs (GDC) were likely to be (which is the cost of purchase and any building costs) and what the gross developmental value (GDV) was projected to be (which is the resale value).

Now the GDV is clearly important to both parties as this indicates the profit the developer will have left after costs and therefore an indicator of how likely you are to get both your fixed interest payment (that's what I'd agreed in this particular instance) and your original capital investment returned. This was supported by a RICS surveyor report (which is not entirely independent as Rupert had instructed the survey but it was still a good thing to have) based on their assessment of the local area for this type of development.

Having received this and thinking it was a good project with all the financials making sense, I forwarded it to both my solicitor and my SSAS administrator advisors.

My solicitor came back with a few comments, quite a few of them negative (speaking to other investors, I get the feeling that this was a fairly common approach from solicitors to this kind of investment), and which basically boiled down to the fact that in his opinion I could lose all my money - or at least most of it. Even though I would have a first charge on the property, it seemed he just didn't like these kinds of deals.

With his comments noted, I politely reminded him he was working for me and that I still wanted to continue with the investment, stating I was an experienced property investor, understood the risks and had undertaken my own due diligence.

The next problem the solicitor had was with the loan agreement document. This was a document my SSAS's administration company had supplied and recommended I use. I shared the draft with Rupert who completed all his sections and I then completed my sections and duly sent this to my solicitor for review.

Oh boy - he was not impressed! He felt there were significant short comings in the document and said he should create one specifically for this purpose.

Now at this point I should point out that part of the agreement I had with Rupert was that he paid for my legal expenses, but up to a limit (they were capped at £2,000). This was to pay for all the standard steps needed to complete the deal and for me to have a first charge on the property. So, when I asked the solicitor how much he would charge for a specific agreement, this was going to almost double the fees my solicitor would charge. This clearly would not be acceptable to Rupert.

In the end and in this instance, I decided to simply ask my solicitor to advise what elements he felt were weak in the loan agreement. He replied with the areas he was concerned about, I created changes to the agreement based on his comments, updated the document and sent it back to him. He was happy with the changes but still felt he should create a new document for me. I decided against it in this instance based on my relationship with Rupert, the developer.

If you were in the same position, you may feel differently and take your solicitors advice and let him create the complete document. Depending on your experience, that should certainly be your first choice as there's absolutely nothing wrong with this approach. If you did, at least you would know you would have a document that totally protects you and could be used for subsequent investments if that's what you planned as part of the strategy to grow your pension fund.

Back to my specific situation, having got all the legals completed and signed on the line, we completed on the purchase and the financing. My SSAS handed over the first payment which would be part of a series of payments or tranches as the project progressed.

This was certainly one good aspect that my solicitor had raised when he highlighted issues with the draft agreement. The original loan document provided by the SSAS Administrators said I would hand over all the funds in one go. My solicitor said it would be better to do this in tranches so that not all my funds were immediately at risk and he also suggested that the developer advise after each payment how the funds had been used. I discussed this with Rupert and he agreed to this approach. So, this was implemented and actually made me feel more comfortable from a risk perspective. It did mean that as I had not forwarded all the required funds in one amount, the percentage return I received in the end was slightly reduced as the interest would become payable on funds drawdown at the time they are drawn down. This is quite conventional with development finance.

Here's the numbers:

GDC - £207,000

GDV - £215,000

Loan Amount - £177,000

Fixed Return on Investment – 12%

This process was really straight forward for me, and Rupert said I could be as active (visiting site, attending some meetings with his project manager) or as passive as I liked, he was totally flexible. In the end I was somewhere in between the two, only visiting site when there was some major progress to be seen as I was quite busy at the time...... writing a book I seem to recall!

Case Study 2 – Care Home Conversion to 3 Terraced Houses

This case study is also from Rupert Green, here he is again to explain more about the property.

"I had purchased the property in 2019. It was a large disused care home in Doncaster and the property had been empty for over 10 years, having fallen into considerable decay due to neglect. It had also been occupied by drug users and other unsavoury types since it had discontinued being a care home. The neighbours were very pleased when I bought the property as the fact it had been empty had resulted in considerable anti-social behaviour over the years, so they were very pleased it was going to be brought back to life and would stop these kinds of issues in the future."

The property was very large and in a great location and most importantly had already obtained planning permission for a conversion from a care home to become 3 residential terraced properties.

Several people in Rupert's network were invited to visit the site to see his latest project, including me. We toured around the site (which seemed huge - I was quite jealous I can tell you) while Rupert explained more about the property and his plans.

"In addition to carrying out the conversion to become three new 4 bedroomed family homes, there is a lot of land at the rear of the property. I feel this could be used to build a detached bungalow if I can obtain the required planning."

This is something you soon realise about Rupert – he doesn't mess about. Not only had he bought a large property for conversion, he saw a further opportunity to maximise the value from the asset by seeking further planning gain to build a further property.

Rupert had secured private lending to purchase the property along with the original planning and that was secured via a first charge on the site. He was now seeking additional funding that would allow the conversion to take place. One of his network had already shown interest in investing in the project with some available funds from their SSAS pension, and had agreed to loan these to Rupert. Now, as there was already a first charge on the site, the best that he could offer as security was a second charge.

This is perfectly acceptable from a SSAS point of view as you don't need to have a first charge when loaning funds from your SSAS to a developer (unlike in a loanback situation where that must be secured with a first charge). This was agreed by the lender for an undisclosed fixed return on investment.

Here are the numbers:

GDC - £519,000

GDV - £590,000

Loan Amount - £265,000

At the time of writing, the site is still in the process of being converted but having seen the drawings, this huge building will be changed into some truly stunning homes. It also inspired me more than ever to want to own my own commercial property. Not necessarily to convert such a building, but it certainly made me see the value of using a SSAS to invest in commercial property. I was so glad when I eventually did.

Chapter 9

Real Estate Investment Trusts (REITS)

REIT's are corporations that own and manage a portfolio of real estate properties. They can focus on one sector (Energy REITs) or be diversified across a number of sectors. Anyone can buy shares in a publicly traded REIT.

The market is a very well-established method for structuring collective investment in UK real estate. It gives the option of investors to plug into a plethora of underlying real estate assets efficiently from rental income streams. Key aspects of REITs include a corporation tax exemption on rental profits and profits from their UK property rental business. REITs must distribute 90% of their net property rental income to investors as a result of these tax breaks.

At the time of writing, there are over 50 REITs with a market capitalisation of around £55 billion listed on the London Stock Exchange investing across a number of sectors. The biggest is industrial and office, followed by diversified (these own and manage a mix of property types, including industrial and commercial), then retail and speciality, with residential and hotel & lodging being the smallest sub-sector.

Normally you would invest in a REIT if you have a longer-term view of the market as these offer little benefit for short-term gains.

Reits Explained

A REIT is just like any other company that you can buy shares in on the stock market. Buying shares in a REIT gives you a part-share holding of ownership of that company. However, unlike normal companies, they differ as they some pretty specific rules they must follow.

To be a REIT, a company has to comply with certain rules, these being:

- Rental income must generate 75% of the company's profit.

- The company's assets must be properties with 75% of them available to rent.
- 90% of the company's rental profit must be paid out to shareholders via dividends.

Since 75% of the company operating profits must come from rental income and 75% of the company's assets must be available for rent, this simply means that we are dealing with a business mainly making their money by buying and renting property. Obviously, this is something that we as real estate investors fully understand and are interested in.

A dividend is a payment from profits that a company makes to its shareholders. A company normally has a lot of discretion about how much of their profits they're paying out. REITs are different because they have to share 90% of their rental property profits to investors each year.

This can be good and bad for the investor. Whilst it means that the investment generates a good annual income, the business is somewhat restricted in opportunities for growth potential as profits cannot be re-invested into other property prospects.

REIT Investment Advantages:

Reliable Income - when renting out to commercial companies the really great thing about rental income is that the renter usually has to sign up for a long lease. That could be anything up to 25 years, with the average length being 8 years[14]. Once this is signed, they are legally obliged to pay the rent until the lease ends or is terminated.

The only way the tenant can get out of it is to sell the contract to someone else (who would have to pay the same rent), by something called a 'break clause' (which enables them to terminate the tenancy in the contract at specified periods) or for the business to go bust.

This means commercial rental income is generally one of the most reliable types of rental income around (unless perhaps you have a large retail portfolio REIT, a sector having a torrid time of late).

Investment Diversification – this is a risk management strategy by allocating investments to different financial instruments, industries and other categories. The aim here is to maximise returns on investment by investing in different segments related to property that could react differently to the same event.

Tax Efficiencies - REITs benefit from some pretty special tax advantages which are useful for a private investor, so here I'm just mentioning it in passing.

At the time of writing, any UK company is required to pay corporation tax on profits at a rate of 19%. This corporation tax is paid by the company before any dividends are paid out to investors.

REITs do not pay any corporation tax.

"But so what", I hear you say, "nor does my SSAS?" I know, I know…. I'm just mentioning it to you as you may want to pass this information on to others that either can't be part of your SSAS, or don't have their own scheme. Because of these tax breaks, it also means there is more money to be shared out in dividend payments to investors.

Liquidity – also as previously mentioned and also in this case, liquidity means it is easy to turn your investment into cash. Just like normal shares, REITs can be sold at any time you want.

REIT Investment Disadvantages

Stock Market - the main one is that you are investing in one business (albeit with diversified property) via the stock market. So, when the stock market as a whole goes down, rightly or wrongly, listed REITs may decrease as well for no logical reason.

Investment Returns from REITs

You receive gains from REITs in two ways:

1. Income from dividends, which is normally paid quarterly
2. Selling shares for a profit from the capital gains

Dividend payment reliability for a given REIT is most likely to be linked to its underlying assets. For this reason, you can probably expect more variation in dividends from a REIT storage company (as this will be more closely linked to how the general economy performs), than one that earns rental income by renting properties to large corporate businesses on long-term leases.

It follows that the value of the REIT shares (and therefore, capital gains) is driven by the prices of commercial property. If the value of the property portfolio increases, then you could possibly expect to see an increase in the share price as well. Conversely, if the portfolio value decreases, then the REIT share value decreases as well.

There is potentially one drawback about investing in a REIT (and it receiving those tax breaks we've already mentioned). For a typical business, it gets to choose what proportion of its profits it wants to pay out as dividends each year. If it wants to grow, it will probably not pay out a large dividend as it wants to invest those funds in business growth. For most businesses, re-investing profits in this way is how businesses grow over time.

Because of the 90% dividend requirement, REITs cannot expand in exactly the same way as regular businesses. That remaining 10% leaves little available spare cash to reinvest in new properties. Because of that, even the best run REITs will be limited in their potential for growth.

Dividends

Because a REIT has limited funds to reinvest in the business and thus grow the share price value, dividend yield is probably the most important consideration for long term REIT investors.

It's worth bearing in mind some things to consider with dividend yields:

- Previous years dividends are no guarantee that they will be at the same level, or even higher, in future years.
- Most companies generally seek to maintain a fixed dividend but this can be harder for REITs because of the 90% payment rules. This means there may be more volatility in the dividend payments.

Effect of Interest Rates

Investors like you need to measure risk and obviously you would want a comparatively higher reward when you see higher risks. Let's assume a hypothetical investor will get a 2% return every year by holding their money in a bank saving account (which is about as secure as investments get...we did see banks fail during the credit crunch in 2007/08, but it's very rare and since then the UK government now guarantees some savings).

It follows in this situation that the investor will want to receive a return of more than 2% for investing in a REIT and they may figure that the additional risk they take on with the investment requires a return of at least 2% more than their savings account. They are therefore looking to invest in a REIT that yields at least 4%.

Now let's say that interest rates go down by 1% (it seems that's the only way interest rates have gone for years), the savings account now offers a 1% return, so the investor only needs a yield of 3% from their REIT based on the previous criteria. In such a situation, a 4% yielding REIT is even more attractive than it was before. Many investors think the same way so the price of the REIT may increase in this situation. Of course, if this was reversed i.e. interest rates went up, then the investor will want a higher yielding investment and may decide to sell.

From this example you can see that as interest rates decrease, the relative value of a REIT is likely to increase. This is what makes REITs quite attractive in the current climate of interest rate declines.

LTV

Loan to values are just as important to REITs as they are to standard commercial loans and mortgages.

Some of the major benefits of currently investing in property is flexibility and relative borrowing cheapness. Borrowing helps property owners to buy land they would otherwise not be able to manage.

The LTV ratio is especially significant during times of declining real estate prices. That is because banks prefer to stipulate a maximum LTV ratio when providing loans to businesses. When the LTV ratio reaches the threshold, then the bank may demand that the borrower, in this case the REIT, pay back some of the loan to reduce the LTV ratio to an appropriate level.

Should the REIT not have the cash available, they could be pushed into selling property or seeking additional capital, all of which are likely to result in a loss of value for current investors.

If a REIT has particularly over-reached itself by borrowing too much, either in or just before a downturn, then they could ultimately face going bust which will result in any investments in the REIT being made worthless.

Investment Risks

As with any kind of investment, there are risks.... especially here as we are dealing with the stock market which we've already mentioned. What other risks might we want to consider with a REIT? Well the main one is property price falls.

With REITs you are ultimately investing in buildings. In the UK we have seen excellent growth in values when you consider this over a long time period. But we all know there have been periods where investors have suffered big losses if they've been under pressure to sell when the market was down.

Should property prices decrease, it is highly likely the value of a REIT will also decrease, along with the share price which can probably be expected to follow suit.

Many REITs own commercial property and land, rather than residential properties. Historically, commercial real-estate prices have been more unpredictable than residential house prices. This is because when an economic downturn occurs, homeowners still need to live somewhere. If companies scale back or even collapse, the industry will suffer a sudden loss of demand.

Market Corrections

As you are now aware, when you buy a REIT you are buying a share in a company listed on the stock market. As we have seen both in 2008/9 and more recently in 2020 with Covid-19, stock markets can perform erratically.

How investors feel plays a big part in how the stock market operates and sometimes those feelings can be completely wrong. This means that even if the REIT you've invested in has been bought at a good price and the REIT has invested well, with all the properties rented out to good paying tenants on long leases, your investment could go down. Why?

Well just like other shares, big price movements in some sectors (like the oil market) can have a big impact on the wider stock market. The result of such moves is that the price of the REIT can get caught up in these unrelated market sectors when nothing has changed in the fundamentals of the investment.

Buying REITs

REITs are shares quoted on the stock market just like normal ones. You can make investments through any of the normal brokers or other broking houses dealing online.

As an aside, if you have an ISA you can even purchase REITs for extra tax benefits within your ISA package. An ISA is a tax-free savings account that comes in different forms, so you'd want a stocks and shares ISA to invest in REITs. The government allows you to invest up to £20,000 a year in ISA stocks and shares and all gains and dividends earned within the ISA are tax-free[15].

We covered quite a lot of criteria in Chapter 5 about buying and selling shares and much of that information is relevant to buying a REIT. The only thing to reiterate here is that REITs are definitely a long-term investment and are probably not worth considering if you want your money out in the short term.

I have not included any case studies on REITs as the process would be very similar to the steps you would use to buy stocks as we've already seen in Chapter 5, so there seemed little point in covering the steps here.

Chapter 10

Hotels and Care Homes

A hotel and care home are regarded by HMRC as commercial property despite the fact that people are obviously staying or living in the property for a period of time, albeit for a limited period.

Let's consider both hotels and care homes as a potential investment opportunity but I will consider each of these in turn and then I will compare the two options.

Hotel Investments

Hotels can be a perfectly viable and tax efficient pension scheme investment, except when a virus comes along and stops everyone travelling.

For hotels you need to make sure that any investment meets the criteria for being classed as a hotel, so as not to fall foul of HMRC requirements. Also, it is quite natural to think of foreign holidays when you consider hotels and there may be some territories (like the Channel Islands) 'considered' British but outside of the UK where you could technically invest using your SSAS. But there are some quite onerous steps needed to achieve an acceptable (to HMRC) investment, and therefore I am going to completely ignore any consideration for hotel investment outside of the UK.

Investment could of course be outright ownership of the entire hotel but you will either be running the business yourself or outsourcing the management to a third party with all the costs this would incur. It could also be a shared ownership of the entire hotel with, for example, the sponsoring employer of the SSAS.

A very important aspect is whether a pension scheme's investment in a hotel carries rights of use for the scheme members. Schedule 29A of the Finance Act 2004 is quite clear that both of the following situations would make the investment a residential property and hence incur tax charges:

- Ownership of part of the hotel (say, one room) but most importantly where it gives the right of a person to occupy that room, or any other part of the hotel; or

- Timeshare rights in the hotel, (for example, the right to stay there for two weeks every August), even where an arrangement allows the person to exchange these rights for accommodation anywhere else in the world.

Of course, it would seem reasonable that you do not have the 'right to occupy' a room if you can only stay there when it's vacant and you also pay the going rate for occupying it.

A hotel room investment clearly differs from a standard commercial property investment. The first difference is the accessibility of the investment, as it's possible to invest in just a single room rather than a whole building as you would normally need to do.

In considering this type of investment in comparison to other multi-occupancy commercial buildings (like an office block) and the size of the investment needed, it would seem obvious that this allows many more investors to participate in the sector due to the much smaller levels of investment needed. Hotel investments have historically been considered as relatively low risk before the Covid-19 virus reared its head. A number of the largest hotel providers are often seeking investment for further developments.

The return on investment rates have been historically high and, as an investor, the contract will often stipulate a buy-back option at a set percentage for the room. If you can, you should ideally look for a contract with an optional buy-back, which means that if the investment gives you good returns, you can retain that for a long-term profit rather than being forced to give up ownership of the asset.

As already mentioned, this process can be entirely passive for you with you simply making the investment, focusing on other aspects of your pension portfolio and collecting the income.

Depending on the investment type, it is usual for the hotel to either take a percentage of the income from your hotel room(s), or for you to take a percentage of the hotel's overall income. Like all investments, it's important to carry out your own due diligence on the hotel you intend to invest in and the company who intends to run the hotel.

Another thing to consider as part of the investment criteria is RevPAR. RevPAR (revenue per available room) is a recognised performance metric in the hotel industry, and this is calculated by dividing a hotel's total guestroom revenue by the room count and the number of days in the period being measured, but it is not an indicator of those hotels likely profitability as it does not include expenses. I'm not going to get into the details of this here but just be aware of it.

Just as there are different types of travellers and customers, there are different types of hotels to cater for each of them from budget to luxury hotels. In a downturn or other difficult financial times, it would seem to make sense that the luxury end of the market would be the most robust to any market softening as their customers have the most disposable income. That said, lifestyle & boutique hotels are also worth considering and look set to continue to grow in the future.

Demand

Growth in hotel room rates (charged prices) has been good in the past with people historically travelling at record levels. In 2019 Frank Knight released data that showed there was £6bn worth of investment in this sector[16]. This report is worth a detailed review if this type of investment interests you, but this was obviously all before Covid-19 impacted the travel industry.

The demand for hotel rooms was on the rise pre Covid-19. In January 2020 the UNWTO World Tourism Barometer was reporting that international tourist arrivals continued to outpace the economy, growing 4% in 2019 to reach $1.5 billion, based on data reported by destinations around the world[17]. It had also expected a growth of 3% to 4% in international tourist arrivals worldwide in 2020....but all this was to become wishful thinking.

What about the risks posed by Airbnb? It seems reasonable to be concerned that the rise of this kind of service provision has affected hotels, and it has. That said, it would appear that Airbnb had almost no impact of the RevPAR figure for hotels[18]. This suggests that Airbnb is offering more of a supplementary service to the hotel industry rather than direct competition, therefore it's unlikely that Airbnb will have a significantly negative impact on a hotel room investment.

One key element that needs to be considered with hotel investments is that you are investing in something that is seasonal. We all recognise there are usually busy periods for travelling, often dictated by children's school holidays (except for December for obvious reasons), especially for tourism. This is something that can be easily overlooked when making an investment in a hotel, so you need to anticipate this. Trying to find a location that is consistently busy all year can be quite challenging.

Risks

As we encounter and state so many times in this book, you are more often than not investing in a business, so your revenue (and profits) as an investor directly correlate to the success of the hotel itself.

The returns on such an investment can be affected in many ways, including the economy, terrorism fears in the area (London has been the subject of a number of attacks), natural disasters (flooding comes to mind in particular in recent years in the UK) and finally as we all now realise, virus infections restricting travel for the general population.

When investing in hotels, you are also investing in the management team who run the hotel. If they decide on a change of strategy, regardless of whether you agree or not, there is little you can do about it. For instance, the hotel may see an opportunity to target a particular customer sector. If this fails, the failure is shared with you as an investor.

As with any property there will be costs to maintain the building and there will also be service charges from the team running the hotel (just like your get service charges on a residential flat). With standard commercial buildings you don't normally see such service charges unless you are using a managing agent. All these costs will be deducted from your income. Make sure you get a full breakdown so you understand what these management costs are. If you don't understand something – ask. Think of yourself as 'Chairman of the Board' and you want your management team to explain what they are spending the company money on.

A potential positive is that hotels don't generally get shutdown, unlike a care home can for poor healthcare provision or abuse. That said you need to make a comparison of the risks and likely returns of this type of investment versus other acceptable SSAS investments.

For myself, I had been tempted to invest in hotels when I was exploring opportunities for using my SSAS funds in the early days, having then recently created the SSAS. Rather than invest in just a room, I was going to hand over a sizeable sum to a company who manages hotel development and refurbishments, and subsequently puts a team into the hotel to manage it on behalf of one of the large hotel chains. I did my initial due diligence and it looked an interesting prospect, but in the end, I decided against it. Not because the investment made me nervous (the management team behind the business seemed very credible), but because I realised I would not be in control of my investment – I was in effect handing over control of my funds to someone else once again (having been in this position when I'd previously had a SIPP). This I decided was not the way I wanted to manage my SSAS.

With hindsight and the situation we all now find ourselves in because of Covid-19 (this being the total shut down of the travel industry and hotels remaining empty), I think it turned out to be a very good decision.

Having said that, we will absolutely get over this virus issue (be it through a vaccine or herd immunity) so don't rule out a future investment in this area. Just consider the risks highlighted by the events of 2020, as part of the overall due diligence that you would carry out before you invest in such a sector. A hotel investment could well be the investment for you, just be sure to do your own research.

Care Home Investment

People all over the developed world and in the UK are now living longer than ever, but with older age comes more strain on public healthcare systems. Therefore, it would appear that investing in care homes (or even a room in a care home which is possible) could be a safe long-term option for securing a regular income for a pension scheme.

Similar to hotel room investments, care home investments offer a share of care home profits but without the huge upfront cost (or more importantly the considerable difficulty) of running such an operation on your own. As care homes are commercial assets and just like all commercial properties, there's no stamp duty tax to pay below £150,000 and the returns can be high if a good location with high fees is selected[19].

Here's how a typical investment might work:

- You buy a room in a care home for let's say £59,000 with the appropriate title deeds.
- The room is leased back to the care home, who now rent it out to their residents and manage it on your behalf.
- You get a fixed rent from the room minus expenses, which

is usually paid monthly or quarterly.

- The deal may also offer an option for the care home to buy your room back at a date in the future providing you with an exit strategy.

In 2017 alone, it was reported by Knight Frank that investors put £1.32 billion into UK healthcare real estate[20]. There are a number of major care home providers in the UK, many with an excellent reputation. Separately reported by Savills, good quality care homes with modern facilities are likely to have full or near full occupancy whilst they are operating[21].

The great thing about the care home industry is that it's regulated by the Care Quality Commission, which means you can check the standard of a care home very easily online. If it has a high rating, it's potentially a good indicator of the management team behind it. Remember, a care home is a business and just like any business it's run by people who will decide if it's a financial success.

While some care home investments specialise in niche areas of care (such as those for people with dementia for example), the sector has a few advantages over buy-to-let. As well as generating higher returns than you'll find in a savings account, one of the biggest benefits to an investor is that care for many residents is funded by the government. This can be very attractive if you're looking for a secure and stable source of income for obvious reasons.

Demand

With advances in medicine, we're living longer and longer than ever. The latest UK data showed that we are likely to live to a ripe old age, this being nearly 83 years old for women, and 79 for men[22]. Whilst these figures occasionally plateau, they are very likely to continue to rise as time rolls on incessantly.

It is also an unfortunate fact that because so many people do not look after themselves and their own health (a result of which is that their bodies start to fail), the more care they will need as the aging process continues. We can see this very clearly in the UK where we have a significant social housing crisis and it seems there just aren't enough rooms to meet demand.

According to analysis by L.E.K. (a global management consulting firm) in 2018, they reported that "in order to address the shortage of care home places, the sector is estimated to need another 200,000 private and public beds over the next 10 years"[23]. This is an interesting report and well worth a read if you are considering this type of investment.

More reports from Age UK show that because 17% of the UK population consists of over 65s, there is a higher demand than ever for care home establishments[24]. Such growth is reported to be partly driven by the number of over 85s, a group expected by the NHS Confederation to double from a figure of 1.5 million in 2014 to 3.6 million by 2039.

As a result of this high demand and low supply, property investors who are considering looking outside their normal areas of buy-to-let investments will consider adding care property to their investment portfolio.

Other positives are that the aging population is much wealthier than it used to be, meaning these people are more willing to pay for private care. Naturally privately funded care is more expensive; than publicly funded care and consequently has seen more investment.

This would certainly suggest that, just based on the expected demand, care homes are potentially worth considering as part of your investment portfolio, if they suit your personal circumstances.

Risks

Investing in new builds of anything always makes me nervous and investing in a new build care home would not make it any easier for me, so make sure you are clear on the protection that is in place to cover deposits. You can also invest in an existing operation that's to be upgraded as some companies look to buy up existing care homes that are underperforming (perhaps due to poor management or a lack of modern facilities) and to turn the operation around. By refurbishing the building and installing better management, these can be returned to a profitable and appealing property for the residents. Because of this, such businesses may be able to be obtained at low prices and turned around to make potentially higher profits.

That said, part of the due diligence in this situation should consider checking the room(s) valuation (was this independent and based on what assumptions?), the performance history of the management or business team and investigating the level of local supply and demand for care in the area. All of this will be key to a successful investment.

Also, just like buying any other commercial property you would invest in, the same factors to consider when purchasing a care home/room apply, these being the location and age of the property.

You need to ensure that there is a positive profitable trading performance from the home and business, that there are good lease terms for the arrangement, understand the tenant covenant strength (which in this instance is basically a tenant with a good reputation for paying) and what the rent cover is. All this needs to be considered as part of your due diligence.

Just like there is in the residential property sector, there is also a market for distressed care home assets and older properties. These are undoubtedly available at softer yields and more affordable prices. Many investors who are looking at this type of product are seeking angles to add value or take a view on the market against the risk associated with that asset and yield applied. Clearly one option with these kinds of properties is for a conversion to residential (as we saw in the case study in Chapter 8), but this would entail obtaining planning permission as this type of conversion is not currently pre-approved under permitted development rights. The property would also need to be sold prior to being certified as habitable at the latest, otherwise there will be tax implications for the pension scheme.

Therefore, care homes are likely to continue to be popular with investors due to strong demand and a small number of new care homes coming onto the market, which eventually would push higher prices and increase yields. The UK care home market for over 65s does not follow a prescribed model. This is a relatively fragmented sector offering a rich and varied mix of businesses and therefore offers a range of opportunities. But it is crucial to ensure that the home/portfolio has solid underlying fundamentals to sustain the investment value in the future, and generate higher returns.

Now having said all of the above, with this type of product you are investing in one property (or even one room), one location and one management team. We have all seen news reports of care homes being closed because of abuse being exposed or generally poor performance (no doubt these are the exceptions), and if you happened to invest in such a care home, your options to exit with your investment are undoubtedly limited.

If you want to greatly reduce your risk but still want to invest in the care sector, an appropriate REIT as mentioned earlier may help you sleep better at night as this will spread your risk with such an investment.

People want to exit investments for all sorts of reasons. It may be possible to sell your care home investment online as they are rising in availability, however a care home room should be considered a long-term investment and not something you can sell easily or at short notice. This should be considered as part of your approach as the investment will likely be illiquid like all property purchases.

Again, and as frequently mentioned throughout this book, due diligence of the specific business economics is crucial, as you'd not only be buying a piece of real estate, but also into the underlying business too. Assuming you have carried out a good analysis and chosen well, care home investments can offer further diversification to your SSAS pension portfolio.

The stability and security of income paid by government funding is hard to ignore and by investing in this way you could be helping to supply care to the many who need it, especially if the investment is locally based as you'll then be supporting your local community with the services it offers.

If you really do need to exit your investment, you'll have to find a suitable buyer who is interested or possibly see if the care business owner would consider buying your investment from you. Remember if you are in a desperate need to sell, the buyer may not be in such a hurry unless there's a good incentive to make the purchase. Considering the worst-case scenario, you may get back less than you invested so buy wisely.

Comparing a Care Home with a Hotel Investment

If you are considering investing in a hotel or care home, it's clear they both provide a similar passive investment for your pension fund. It also allows for the further diversification of your investment portfolio through this route. Both types of investment will probably provide similar returns and are also of a similar price to purchase. In either case, the investment will be secured with title deeds.

The two main differences between them are i) the amount of rooms in the building (a fairly typical care home will be around 25 rooms, where as a typical hotel might have 100 rooms) and ii) the length of time that a person will stay at the property. The occupancy of a hotel room might be on average 2-3 days, whereas the occupancy of a care home might typically be 3 or more years, with this increasing with good quality care and increasing life expectancy.

On the face of it, there is very little to choose between the two......that was until Covid-19 came along and took a great bite out of the travel industry. With recent events, they will no longer be considered to be as similar in nature as they once were.

When you think about it, Covid-19 could be considered the ultimate 'black swan' event for this (and other) markets. Rarity, extreme impact and retrospective predictability are considered three of the characteristics of a black swan event. Black swan events come out of nowhere to derail financial markets and these events are apparently called this because of an old saying that black swans did not exist, until one appeared out of nowhere to prove they did.

It is therefore pretty easy from this recent perspective of the virus outbreak to draw conclusions about which of the above offers the best investment vehicle for your SSAS funds. One thing we have clearly seen in 2020 with Covid-19 is that hotels remained empty due to travel lockdowns, but care homes had to continue operating.

I personally have been tempted to invest in hotels but in the end I didn't and now I'm very glad I didn't. That said, whilst there is an undoubted need for care homes, these can easily be shut down by the authorities due to poor management in the care provided.

You can see that both of these investments carry some level of risk…. and of course you are not in control of your investment asset. But if you do want a passive investment (as there is generally no involvement from the investor in either of these options), both offer that opportunity.

If I was forced to choose, I know which route I'd probably go down but that may not be the same for you. Ultimately, it's down to you as a SSAS trustee to make the decision if this kind of investment is for you, so seek suitable advice from your trusted advisors.

Chapter 11

Buying Land and Forestry or Woodland

Buying land with your SSAS is perfectly acceptable but it's important to consider the potential financial viability of such an investment.

An example is buying an agricultural plot and then leasing it to a farming business. Other alternatives could include equine centres, commercial forestry, forestry, camping and glamping sites etc.

Many of you will have heard the bad reputation that land banking gets. This is where you see segregated parcels of land being sold in the potentially vain hope it might get planning permission. These are often in green belt areas where the likelihood of this being achieved are remote to say the least, and are even considered to potentially be scams[25.]

That said, it is perfectly reasonable to buy land in the expectation (based on some form of logic) that at some point in the future (maybe not your future but that of your children or grand-children), the land obtains planning permission. It could be a parcel of land that is between some commercial or residential developments and is not used in any way. Alternatively, you could select land that you have an immediate plan for in how you'd use it.

As with all the investments mentioned in this book, the appropriate amount of due diligence is required. This includes the argument for the purchase, and speculative land purchases are obviously high risk and would offer little sound commercial justification for the investment. Such a purchase may result in little capital growth or you may find after a failed planning application you cannot sell the land. Again, you need a plan B if your initial reason for buying the land hits the buffers. Equally your SSAS buying a piece of land at the end of your garden is not really a serious use of your funds.

For land purchases, you should ensure that a number of elements are clearly defined. These include:

- That the land has clearly defined borders or boundaries.
- There is good access to the land from a public road and that it is not land-locked (no direct access).
- There is a clear legal title to the land.
- There is no tangible moveable property included in the purchase price (such things would need to be separately funded).

Buying Residential Land

A SSAS can purchase land that has been zoned for residential development as long as it does not contain any building or structure which is suitable for use as a dwelling. Here the SSAS could obtain planning for residential property and then sell the land to a developer or develop the land itself and then sell it before habitation is certified.

We will speak at length about the risks of the SSAS being seen to be trading (which a scheme must not do) in Chapter 14. Therefore, you need to be aware that if the pension buys the land outright for residential development, you may only get one shot at this kind of approach. Clearly, developing the land for commercial reasons would present no such issues.

Buying Woodland or Forestry Land

For investments in woodland or forestry, you are quite limited in the UK. For such investments, the main income benefit comes from the sale of the timber itself.

Unfortunately, trees, in this instance, would probably be classed as tangible movable property and this means it would not be acceptable as a SSAS investment. Equally, by selling the wood after the trees were felled, the scheme would be considered to be trading and again this is not acceptable.

Thus, a potential option to get involved in woodland or forestry investment would be from buying the land and leasing it to someone who wanted to grow trees on the land. They would handle all the business side of things and therefore the SSAS simply has an investment that it receives a fair rental income from.

Even if you can find some land that someone is willing to lease from you to grow tress on, it's worth knowing that returns for your tenant are generally only paid once the trees can begin to be harvested and the timber sold. This usually occurs 4-6 years into the investment so you'll need an experienced tenant that will be able to pay their lease for a long period before they see any income themselves.

Chapter 12

Combining Pension Funds into a SSAS

There are 3 main types of approaches when it comes to combining or pooling pension funds into a SSAS:

1. Combining all your own personal pension pots.
2. Combining pension pots within a family (husband and wife, adult children).
3. Combining pension pots of non-related people.

Let's look at each of these in turn.

Combining your Own Funds

If you've had a diverse and perhaps somewhat transient career where you've worked at several different employers, you may have several pension pots dotted around that remained with the business when you left their employment. You may have even forgotten about them, which is why it's always a good idea to think about all the places you've worked at for a period of time and seeing if there is a pension pot (however small) sitting there waiting to be collected.

Combining pension pots all together into a single SSAS is an ideal way to consolidate your funds, and surprisingly those small funds can add up to a reasonable sum when combined together.

Combining Family Funds

It's quite possibly the case that a family who has a business will be running it based just on the founders. The business owners may have even worked for a previous employer where they have contributed to a pension scheme. Any adult children or other family members may or may not be working in the business. In either case it's possible they have also been paying into a pension of their own, either through a private pension, or perhaps a pension set up by their employer.

In this situation, there is the opportunity for the family to place their money together into one pension scheme e.g. a SSAS. It's basically the same approach as the first method we discussed, this being where a single person consolidates their own pension pots, but now the family are consolidating their pension pots all together.

As the family will have a business in some form (acting as the sponsoring employer), by pooling their pension assets into a single SSAS, the funds can be used for business growth or another type of investment if that's what the trustees want to do…and of course, all the funds are protected in the event of a member's death. For balance, a similar objective can also be achieved using a family pension trust or family SIPP.

As the scheme's members will have different amounts to transfer in, the scheme administrator will need to record these different amounts to calculate each person's share of fund. As and when contributions are made to the scheme, the share of fund will need to be recalculated to ensure at any point each member is aware of how much belongs to them. This can be quite complex and is why I recommend that using a professional scheme administrator is so important.

So, by pooling together the respective funds, the SSAS has more financial muscle than the individual funds would have had by themselves.

There is another benefit of this arrangement, although no one wants to think of the worst-case scenario.

When one of the members unfortunately dies, which is inevitable, the SSAS will be able to continue unimpeded. It won't be necessary to sell any of the assets held in the scheme as they are effectively passed to the other beneficiaries. This would mean that these funds can remain invested, whichever form that takes, within the scheme. If no income is needed at that time, it can continue to grow until it is needed, or until it is passed to another beneficiary on a further member's death.

Combining Non-Related People Funds

The process here is very similar to combining a family fund except that the people in the SSAS are unrelated. You can have up to 11 people in a SSAS pension scheme and none of them need to be related.

Now I think it would be quite unusual to see this situation, it's much more likely that you will see a group made up of some related people combining their money with some (very well-known to them) unrelated business connections. Remember right at the start I said running a SSAS is like running a business, well using business connections in this way could possibly strengthen the use of your SSAS funds. Clearly you would not (or should not) enter into a business arrangement with someone you don't know that well and this is the same situation. Combining your pension funds with other people is an intricate process and extracting yourself from such an arrangement could be convoluted to say the least.

Methods of Consolidating Pension Pots

There are a number of methods to combine pension pots together. We'll now go through the various ways this can be done.

In Specie Transfers

'In specie' is a Latin term meaning 'in the actual form' but basically this simply means transferring the ownership of an asset to another entity e.g. a person or company, in its current form. In other words, you don't need to sell the asset to release its cash value prior to a transfer.

In specie transfers can involve shares, property or funds and in our case, it simply means transferring it from another pension scheme to our SSAS.

In specie transactions can be credited to pension schemes in two different ways – in specie transfers and in specie contributions. Let's look at an in specie transfer first.

This is the transfer of an asset from one pension scheme to another. Let's assume that a member of a pension scheme has a SIPP and, after taking advice from a suitably qualified financial advisor, decides he or she wants to transfer everything from this scheme to their newly created SSAS pension. Checks on the transfer will be carried out by the scheme administrator and/or accountant of the new SSAS arrangement and they will confirm that it will accept the transfer of assets.

For an in specie contribution, this involves the movement of an asset from an individual or company to a pension scheme. This is where, rather than making a cash payment to a pension scheme, assets such as property or shares are 'paid' into the scheme instead. This moves the asset ownership to the pension scheme. The asset would not have previously been in another pension fund (so can't be transferred), so ownership would have existed outside of a pension scheme. If the asset was already in a pension scheme, this would then be an in specie transfer.

Share Transfers

If you simply sell the shares that were perhaps held in a SIPP, you can then move the resulting funds from one account to the SSAS account.

I actually did this with some shares I held in a SIPP…the fund had performed badly and had lost money versus the original investment (note to self - don't leave my finances to faceless advisors).

But the shares you have may be a really good investment and you don't want to sell them.

Here your SSAS trustees must ask for an in specie transfer from the original scheme to your SSAS. Paperwork naturally needs to be completed to request this, and at the same time gives the SSAS or scheme administrator authority to contact the original scheme to arrange the transfer. The original scheme administrator will then arrange the transfer but be aware this may take some time to complete the process.

Property Transfers

As property involves things like title deeds, you will need a solicitor to be involved in this process as well as the scheme administrator.

The SSAS trustees will request the scheme's solicitor to contact the current owner's legal representative with a request to move the property into the scheme. The SSAS should carry out the normal conveyancing searches, checks and independent valuation just as if it were purchasing the property off the open market. Obviously, for a transfer of this sort, it cannot include any taxable property e.g. residential.

Here is a case study of a family that have combined their pension funds into a single SSAS.

Case Study - Combining Pension Funds

The Thomas family have been running their own family business for many years. It was started by Ron and Hilary and eventually their two sons, Lee and Patrick, joined the company after careers away from the family business. Being in control of your own business can be very rewarding, especially when it is so successful, but protecting it should Ron and Hilary die was something they had recently started to think about.

Following a conversation with a financial advisor, they became aware of the benefits of setting up a SSAS and combining their pension pots.

"Both Lee and Patrick had their own pensions from their previous employer" explained Ron, "and both I and Hilary fully expect to hand over the business to Lee and Patrick at some point. Following the discussion with the financial advisor, it seemed to make sense for both the boys and us to combine all our pension money into a SSAS to help grow the business. It was explained that by doing this, the funds can be used for the business and additionally are protected in the event of our death."

With their sons now driving the business forward, they wanted to expand and needed a bigger premises to support this projected growth. The whole family were concerned that, as Ron and Hilary were getting older and the boys were also dependant on the business, getting a loan agreed from the bank might be difficult to achieve. They also didn't want to continue to rent a building as they currently did, as they wanted the security of adding value to a building that they would benefit from in the long term. It was also just at this time that a break clause in their lease was coming up, so this was an ideal time for them to leave their current rented premises.

"Both me and Hilary had been employed by other business before we set up the company, which meant we had some pensions in other places. The boys also had some small pensions that we discovered could be combined into a single SSAS if they wanted to."

After taking advice and having discussed it at length, the family decided to establish a SSAS with the business as the sponsoring employer. Having set the scheme up, it was agreed that this would be initially funded by combining all the family's pension schemes into one, making them all trustees.

"With all the pensions combined, we were now in a position to go shopping for a commercial building that we could buy with the SSAS funds. This was great as it would really allow the business to grow and be something that the boys could get their teeth into."

They subsequently found a suitable premises that the SSAS purchased outright and this was then leased to the business at a commercial rate. This actually meant they would be effectively renting it from themselves, whilst having this as a business expense for the company P&L.

"The SSAS has given us the ability to fund business growth without borrowing from the bank at higher rates. This has given us greater flexibility to support the business expansion plans, but we wouldn't have been able to do this without bringing all the various pension plans together."

Chapter 13

Student Halls of Residence

This is another exception to the rule of holding property where people reside or are residents.

Yes, it's another type of 'residential property' that is allowed and this is for students.

"Hurrah!" I hear all those HMO student property owners chanting. But wait, you need to get the full picture as there are strict caveats that decide whether it is or is not an acceptable purchase for investment purposes with your SSAS.

There is clearly a variety of accommodation that is available to students, from standard homes to HMO's specifically catering for this market. In deciding if a student accommodation property can become an asset in your SSAS, it's vital to look at what type of property it is and if it has a formal connection to an educational establishment.

To be clear right from the get-go, HMRC will not consider an individual house let to students as a hall of residence, nor will they consider a standard HMO property as suitable. The key wording is that for it to be acceptable and thereby exempt from being classed as a standard residential property, it needs to be a 'hall of residence'.

So what does that mean?

To meet the required HMRC criteria, it's necessary to be guided by them in this situation. They state that to be a hall of residence, a property needs to be connected (by arrangement of identification, not necessarily owned by the establishment or physically on its campus) to a specific educational establishment and provide accommodation on a communal basis for students of that establishment only.

The educational establishment needs to be involved in placing students in the building. "Ok" you might say, "that should not really be an issue as they do this all the time."

Well now the difficult bit.

There are restrictions on the configuration of the property for the students and this is the killer blow for many SSAS pension trustees thinking that can invest in this particular market sector as I will now show you.

The layout requires for there to be common living areas or eating/cooking facilities or services, and these must be provided for the use of all the occupants.

"Right, well that's still ok - so far, so good."

At this point it's worth me mentioning that I have a number of HMO residential student properties in university towns. Over the last few years, I have seen in these towns that there has been a considerable drive by developers building new purpose-built student accommodation. Many of these properties have wonderful self-contained layouts effectively creating mini-apartments, with a kitchen and bathrooms (some of these being ensuite) for the exclusive use of, say for example, the 6 students living in that apartment. No one would have to leave the apartment to go to the kitchen or bathroom and this means they are completely self-contained…and herein lies the problem.

To meet HMRC's requirements, for it to be classed as student halls, the property must not be segregated into self-contained apartments with one or more bedrooms.

This is the killer blow preventing many SSAS pensions being able to invest in student accommodation. Hallways with several small bedrooms coming off them, with a tiny desk to study and one kitchen and one bathroom for the whole corridor to use are things that are now the stuff of legend.

Students now want their own bathroom, bedroom, place to study and eat and to be able to make their own choice if they want to socialise or not. Going back to my own student HMOs, I now have all of them equipped with either ensuites or off-suites (these are bathrooms for one student's exclusive use but they are not accessible directly from within their room). The market changed and I saw that if you don't provide this accommodation level to students, you may struggle to let your property, depending on the demand.

It's also worth mentioning that unlike hotel or care rooms, individual student rooms within a property cannot be purchased or sold separately. If you did, there is the possibility it could be classed as holding property that is used for the enjoyment of residential property and therefore expose the SSAS to tax charges.

If you want to still invest in student accommodation without going through the process of finding a suitable student halls property, there is another route where it would be perfectly acceptable for a SSAS to invest in student accommodation – even in ones just like the new build properties I mentioned earlier. This would be once again through a REIT. In this situation, certain criteria would need to be met, but it would be perfectly acceptable to invest in student accommodation via this route.

I've not provided any case studies for this chapter. If you were to invest in student accommodation using REITs or another fund, you would use a similar process detailed in Chapter 9, so it seemed pointless repeating it here. Also, I could not find anyone that had invested in student halls in recent years. Maybe they are just so outdated now with increased demands from the customers (students) on what they want from a room/apartment that this type of investment seems to have run its course unless HMRC change the rules.

I still thought it worth covering this subject in this chapter as I've heard of quite a few people (a lot in actual fact) thinking that they can use a small residential student HMO with their SSAS. I wanted to discourage that approach immediately, it's just not acceptable due to it being highly likely to be considered a residential property by HMRC.

Chapter 14

Planning Gain and Title Splitting

Another great way to benefit from commercial property investment is buying something that can be converted into a residential property or can be sub-divided into part commercial and part residential. This is done all the time by developers converting large commercial buildings into individual flats or HMOs.

The ease with which it can be converted to residential will also depend on the type of property. Basically, any commercial property can in theory be converted to a residential property but it would obviously need planning permission to do this.

There are certain kinds of commercial property that do not need planning permission as they have something called permitted development rights (PDR). In 2013 the planning rules changed, which meant certain kinds of commercial property could be converted to residential without the need for full planning permission. The UK Government announced in June 2020 that significant and further changes to these rights will come into effect from September 2020.

Only certain commercial properties have PDR and I'm only going to consider a few as they are the most popular, these being:

- A1 shops to C3 Dwelling.
- B1 business to C3.
- B1c light industrial to C3.

Now C3 dwelling is clearly residential property, so you may think this is not acceptable with a SSAS. Well, we will get into this so please read on.

To get planning permission on a commercial property, you would apply to the local council in much the same way you would for a residential property.

You'd need to apply directly to your local council's department of local planning authority (LPA). Application fees vary considerably for change of usage and to obtain full planning approval. Each LPA functions slightly differently so be sure to participate in the process as soon as you can.

Using Permitted Development Rights

What you are allowed to do under PDR has changed several times over the last few years so it's worth checking what is and is not allowed. At the time of writing, the last set of permitted development rights come into force on the 25th May 2019[26]. Boris Johnson announced a big shake up in the planning process and it was expected further PDR changes were to be announced in September 2020, so ensure you check the latest arrangements for PDR[27].

It's important to be mindful that although planning permission is not required, you still need to seek 'prior approval' from your local authority. Prior approval means a developer must seek the local planning authority's approval, and this is to ensure that any specified development elements are acceptable before the work can begin.

Another very important thing to be aware of is that PDR is only allowing the change of use, not the conversion itself. In other words, you might still need planning permission if you need to knock down walls or add an extension. If you intend to stay inside the building fabric without any structural changes, you should be ok to just use PDR.

Like most things, there are always exceptions and this is true for PDR. One definite exception is a listed building. If you plan to convert or develop a building which is listed, you'll most certainly need to go through full planning process. In addition, the LPA might also request full architectural drawings. The standards required for a listed building often go way beyond the requirements for a regular building, so this must be considered as there could be a need to use more expensive materials. Lastly, even if the building is not actually listed, if the commercial property is within a conservation area, a National Park or an area of outstanding natural beauty, this may mean it is also treated as listed with all the additional requirements this entails.

If the property is a leasehold, it probably is not worth (in my opinion) a conversion. That said, people have done this and if you did decide to press ahead and needed a mortgage to complete the conversion, please ensure that at least 70 years are remaining on the lease as this is almost certainly to be a requirement for most lenders. Clearly you will also need the permission of the freeholder before you can begin any work.

It's worth mentioning here that if you are considering a property for development works (even if it's just to increase the size and keep it as a fully functioning commercial building), you may wish to register the scheme for VAT and opt to tax the property, as this would mean the pension fund could reclaim the VAT on the invoices for the building works.

Conversion Options

When it comes to commercial to residential conversions, there are a few types that are particularly attractive to developers. The most popular ones are B1 (office) to C3 (dwelling), B1c (light industrial) to C3.

A1 (Shop) to C3 (Dwelling)

For starters, there are already a wide range of shop retail property for sale, from small high street units to large department store sites. The retail sector in particular had been hard hit during the financial crisis in 2008/9 and was still trying to recover. Now following the latest crisis with Covid-19, there could be a lot more coming onto the market. Retail stores had been in dire straits for years with the growth of the online retailers. I saw a report on BBC news in May 2020 where Theo Paphitis (of Dragons Den fame) said he felt that changes to online retail buying behaviour had been accelerated by 5 years[28]. This would suggest that many retail units could be up for grabs post the virus period.

The place where conversion is potentially most likely to be possible/ desirable is where a unit is within a row of residential properties. This is particularly applicable in places away from town centres. It could have previously been a small hairdressers that is no longer operating with residential above it, or another kind of retail unit with offices for the retail unit above it. Shops with office uppers would immediately mean your SSAS should be able to buy the whole property, unlike shops with residential uppers where it could only buy the commercial retail element.

It is really important that the part of the building to be converted to residential has not previously been used as residential (even if it's now being used as commercial space). HMRC view a commercial building (such as a shop) with an inter-connected residential area (such as a flat) as one building and therefore would deem the whole building as residential. You therefore need to make sure you check the history of the property. The residential part would also have to have a separate entrance.

B1c (Light industrial) to C3

A light industrial conversion probably tops the list for desirability as these kinds of buildings are often already located within residential areas. This immediately makes the conversion perfect to blend in to the area it is located in, making the environment conducive for dwelling. Some of these conversions can be made to look truly stunning when done well. A key thing for this kind of development is that the building changing use must be 500 sqm or less. PD rights are also reviewed frequently, so do check this type of conversion is still allowed as things may have changed since the publication of this book.

B1 (Office) to C3 or Mixed Use (being both B1 and C3)

There has been growing demand for this type of conversion. An office building can be converted to multiple residential rooms with ensuites as part of a HMO. Many residential buy-to-let landlords have been implementing this approach due to higher yields in comparison to single property lettings.

In this situation, the SSAS would be able to buy the property initially (as it is a complete commercial building) and then potentially get it converted. If you turned the entire building into residential, you would need to sell the entire building before it was declared habitable to avoid tax penalties from HMRC for owning taxable property, but this could be a great capital generator for your pension scheme.

Alternatively, you could be buying a commercial building that lends itself to be converted into a mixed-use property. This could mean the building becomes a mix of both commercial and residential use. If you buy the building with your SSAS, you would need to dispose of the residential element before it becomes habitable.

No Trading

Another very important area of caution is that you can't do this too often (or even more than once) otherwise the scheme could be considered to be trading, and this again would get you in hot water with HMRC.

I've spoken with a number of SSAS pension specialists and it seems a very grey area for sure. Some of the general comments I've received said it's a very tricky and an undefined area, and that you would also need to consider the similarity of transactions (doing the same conversion every time) as well as the frequency of the conversions.

Basically, it's down to you and the other scheme trustees, who would need to take a view. Most guidance I received from professional advisors would err on the side of caution (no one wants to be liable for a client's default), saying that they would only allow the scheme to do such a conversion once in the lifetime of the SSAS.

One cautionary comment made to me was that, considering the levels of Government spending recently due to Covid-19 and the amount of tax revenue that could be generated if HMRC decided to start looking into multiple transactions, you really do need to tread cautiously. HMRC do decide occasionally to target specific practices and test the water with a court case and this could potentially be one area they could come to look at.

Next Steps

I do suggest you check with your particular specialist advisor to be guided by what they consider is, and is not, an acceptable process of engaging in such conversions. If they say go ahead, at least if HMRC do come after you, you should be covered by the administrator's professional indemnity insurance.... unless they get you to sign a disclaimer, then you're on your own. You must be guided by your own suitably qualified advisors who are aware of your personal circumstances before embarking on these kinds of investments.

The following case studies show how a SSAS could potentially be used to gain the full benefits of planning gain from a commercial building.

Case Study 1 - Planning Gain

Peter McBain had worked in the tool-making trade all his life. As his experience developed, he eventually set up his own business with a small tool workshop which expanded over the years. As his business grew, he just happened to have a friend who was also an independent financial advisor and this resulted in him setting up a SSAS when they were still relatively unknown.

"Luckily I had a contact from the local pub that was always going on about financial 'this' and financial 'that' and how I should set up this thing called a directors (SSAS) pension. Over several beers we did discuss it quite a lot and when I looked into it, I did think it would be a good thing to establish. So, Derek (the contact from the pub who happened to be a financial advisor) helped me set it up. Seems an age ago now that we did that."

Having the SSAS in place, the available funds in it were used to purchase the company building. This consisted of an office and warehouse which housed the machines and other equipment that were used to manufacture items for the equally small engineering firms in the locality. Some years after buying the commercial building (which he was originally renting), but before he set up his SSAS, he was offered a piece of scrub land of reasonable size adjoining his commercial business as the owner needed some cash at the time.

"There were always people chatting down the pub about business and if there were any opportunities to work together. Another contact of mine mentioned there was some land near my property and he thought the owner wanted to sell. At the time I thought 'what do I want that for?' but there had been some property development in the area. So, somehow, I ended up buying this land privately thinking that maybe one day it would be worth something."

Peter had started to notice changes in the business environment since he first set up the business, particularly from competition. There was also a drive for higher quality in the tooling market with ever greater standards requiring continued investment in the business. He had decided that the time was right for him to consider retiring. With two grown up children, he wanted to ensure that they were supported in their life going forward. They had both become additional trustees of the SSAS about 3 years previously and the tooling business made contributions on their behalf, so they had benefits in their own right.

Peter's wife, Jackie, had also worked for the business for many years and had a sizeable share of the SSAS. They had also made nominations to pass their benefits to their children in the event of their deaths. Whilst they were both in good health, they had decided this was a sensible provision to make.

"It's nice to know that, when we die, the kids can continue to benefit from the income from the property asset without the need for its sale if that's what the kids choose to do."

Next to the warehouse is the piece of industrial scrub land which they bought several years ago in their personal names (not in the limited company name). The land has its own access to the highway, is now adjacent to some existing residential development property, with demand still continuing. Derek (the IFA) suggested that it would possible to transfer the land into the SSAS, perhaps to pursue either commercial or residential planning permission. Now whilst the land had no planning, it had gone up in value slightly since the purchase but not by a significant amount. So, Peter organised an independent survey and valuation to be carried out and subsequently the land was acquired by the pension scheme.

An additional bonus of this step is that the land is then no longer part of Peter and Jackie's estate for inheritance tax purposes, and no longer subject to any capital gains tax should any planning permission be achieved.

Peter and Jackie, along with their children contracted with an architect to draw up possible plans for a development. In discussions they held with him, he advised that going the residential route was likely to be the most profitable in the short term. They all agreed with this and using funds from the SSAS, he was appointed to submit a planning application to the LPA.

"To cut a long story short, the planning application for a small block of residential flats was successful and the land immediately saw an increase in value within the SSAS. This was great but Derek made us aware that the SSAS cannot hold any residential property, so we needed to decide what to do with the land now that it had residential planning."

Peter and Jackie really had no experience of property development or running residential property rentals and neither did the other trustees. Because of this, they decided the simplest thing was to sell the land with planning to a developer. This they did with the help of their legal and financial advisors.

This turned out to be a win-win situation all round.

As a result, the SSAS is free from capital gains and income tax, so the planning gain incurs no tax within the SSAS. Both Peter and Jackie are over the moon to have made such a gain on the land that was standing idle, and even happier that they are not going to pay any tax on the gain.

Whilst they did slightly increase their personal funds when the land was originally sold to the SSAS, this was minimal compared to the increase that would have occurred had they obtained planning with the land in their own name.

Jackie has the last word, "I used to complain that Peter was always down the pub, but I have to say the contacts he's made over the years there have been really useful."

Peter can't help but have a big grin on his face.

Case Study 2 - Mixed Use Property and Title Split

Tony Adams is a small business owner and he occasionally invests in property via his SSAS pension scheme which he had already set up. He also has a small property company which he uses to buy residential property to rent out and to develop new build residential property.

As he had some surplus funds available for an investment in both his SSAS and property business, he had been looking for a commercial building to purchase that he could ideally convert to residential and subsequently rent out to tenants. He'd been looking for some time but just couldn't find something that fitted what he wanted. As a result, he decided to be a bit more flexible in his search and consider something that was of mixed use.

He found just such a property on the market in his local area. The property was being offered on a freehold title basis and consisted of a retail space at street level with a residential flat above. Both the flat and the retail space were empty (due to it being poorly maintained and marketed) and he decided in his plan to place both a commercial and residential tenant into each part of the property. The freehold of the property was valued at £250,000 and the valuation showed this to be roughly equally split between both the residential and non-residential parts.

Tony takes up the story…. "In this situation, the SSAS was not able to purchase any part of the property. This was down to the residential element, which is not permitted as a pension asset. The SSAS could only purchase the non-residential part as, if it was owned by my SSAS, I knew the residential elements 'value' would be classed as an unauthorised payment by HMRC."

"My understanding is that in England and Wales, a freehold title includes all land and buildings above and below the property without limit, but the good thing is that freehold titles can be split."

So how did Tony use his SSAS to invest in this type of property?

"Basically, I needed to find a way that I could use my SSAS funds without it ever being the owner of the residential part of the property. With my solicitors help, we did find an approach but it did become a little complex."

The purchase was made possible by developing an effective buying process and involving his solicitors help right at the early stages. This paid dividends in making the purchase a success and staying the right side of rules with HMRC.

The solution was to create a new leasehold title (this is where the title split element comes in) within the existing freehold title and the process that Tony used was as follows:

- An offer was made to the vendor to purchase the property for £250,000.

- A RICS valuation was carried out by a surveyor to confirm the leasehold title value of the commercial space

- A solicitor was appointed by Tony's SSAS to act on its behalf.

- Legal work was commenced to transfer the freehold title to Tony's property business, but simultaneously the solicitor created a new leasehold title on the non-residential part.

- The freehold title transferred to Tony's property company and a leasehold title was given to the SSAS. The SSAS released £120k to the solicitor and Tony's property business released £130k to the solicitor.

- The seller received £250,000 for the freehold title of their property.

In this situation, there were some key points as to why this worked so well for all concerned. These included:

- The seller saw only one buyer, one offer and one payment which was a much-simplified process from their viewpoint.

- The SSAS became the leasehold title 'owner' of the permitted non-residential retail space (just to be clear, the SSAS is not paying rent to Tony's property business but is the owner of the commercial element outright).

- The SSAS will have no 'interest' in the residential part

- Tony's property business can choose to retain the residential flat to let out or to sell it on to a third party.

"This turned out to be a really good investment for me. My SSAS gained a commercial investment and my property business gained a residential property that was not even on the market. We only spent about £15,000 in refurbishment costs on the shop and the flat combined as all the fundamentals were there, it just was tired and needed bringing up to date."

"The shop is now let to a tenant and so is the flat as I decided not to sell it as I want to continue to build my residential portfolio."

"Now I understand this process of buying a mixed-use property, but I'm aware I need to be cautious so that the pension scheme is not considered to be trading. With that in mind, I would definitely consider doing it again. However, based on the guidance of my professional SSAS administrator, they feel that doing this again is potentially leaving me open to tax charges down the road and they currently wouldn't support doing it again."

Chapter 15

Intellectual Property

Certain assets such as intellectual property (copyrights, patents, and trademarks for example) are intangible and so are not classed as tangible moveable property for a SSAS investment.

Therefore, a SSAS is allowed to invest directly into a company's Intellectual Property (IP). In addition, IP rights is an acceptable form of security for a loanback to the sponsoring employer (just the same as a property would be).

It could easily be the case that a company has a significant amount of IP as a result of the business competitive advantage for the services or products it produces. This can easily be overlooked as it's not something that is normally captured in a business assets – especially in its balance sheet. There have been estimates that IP could represent a significant amount of a company's value, way beyond any physical assets a business may own.

There are various things that could be considered as IP:

- Company brand.
- Database.
- Trade secrets.
- Know how.
- Software.
- Manufacturing methods.
- Patents.
- Product designs.
- Copyright.

The list of items above all go in to making up the business IP assets but these are often undervalued, frequently managed poorly compared with the level of importance that they should be and often not protected properly. I think it would be fair to say that this form of investment is becoming increasingly recognised by many business owners for the value they have for such intangible business assets.

From the list above, let's consider what some of these are.

Patents are probably some of the most valuable assets a business can have. No doubt we've all watched Dragons Den episodes on BBC2 and seen the Dragons' eyes light up when patents are mentioned. The business owner is pitching their business and then happens to mention they hold the patent for the product they are presenting. That's because the Dragons know that if they can hold the patent to a product, it provides them with the right to exclude others from exploiting the patented technology, including, for example, making, using, or selling the patented invention.

One patent that comes to mind for me (as it was one of my former employers) is the electrically heated front screens on Ford vehicles. Quickclear is a European trademark used by Ford for its electrically heated windscreen technology. Ford no longer have exclusivity of this technology but they did for many years.

In some cases, patents can be so innovative that they give the owner a complete monopoly over an entire industry and therefore are extremely valuable, potentially worth billions of dollars.

We've also seen in the news over the years musicians contesting who wrote a song first and therefore who owns the copyright. Royalties are paid to the owner of songs every time it is played on the radio and so this can be a big money earner for the musician. Everyone knows the song "Merry Christmas Everybody" by Slade which it is believed generates around £500,000 in royalties every year[29].

Having worked in the food industry, I know manufacturers of certain food products are extremely secretive of either the recipe or the way a product is manufactured. They know that if a competitor finds the secret of how they produce something, it can be copied and this can be extremely damaging to their sales as they will lose a competitive advantage. This is particularly true if you are quite a small food business and perhaps someone in the family has passed on a secret recipe or method of making something that only the family knows.

Going back to Dragons Den again, we all know the now legendary story of 'Reggae Reggae Sauce' creator Levi Roots (whose real name is disappointingly Keith!). Peter Jones and Richard Farleigh each invested £25,000 for 20% of Levi's business 'idea', and Levi is now estimated to be worth £30 million[30]. The recipe was trademarked in 2007 (when Levi appeared on the show) and even the bottle was trademarked in 2012.

What does all this mean if you have a property business? Well, if you have a property training business that is scaleable and/or is already generating significant revenue, you are almost certain to have an IP asset that could be used as security for a loan. There are several property 'gurus' who are probably making as much money from property training as they are from property. If they are well known enough, they could potentially sell this brand identity to their SSAS (if they had one) and lease it back to their sponsoring employer. This would be a great way of releasing further capital for business growth.

From the above examples, we can see that IP can be very valuable to a business and therefore how it can be something that can be used as security for an investment.

Valuations

It's important to understand that this is a specialised area and it has historically been very difficult to establish accurate valuations for this type of asset, but there are now more specialists that can help in this arena. These specialists are also able to give further advice on how it may be possible to increase the value of the business IP and thus the loan that is possible.

When a business is looking to grow, it might be worth considering exploiting the capital value of its IP and utilising this value in combination with the funds of the SSAS. The way this value can be released is for the business to sell its IP to the SSAS. The SSAS then agrees to lease back the IP back to the company at a commercial rate.

This means the business gets an injection of capital (in just the same way it would from a loanback) to further aid its expansion. Another benefit is that as the IP is now held within the SSAS, should the business fail for any reason, the IP is protected from any creditors.

So, the SSAS is receiving a regular tax-exempt income for leasing the IP to the business and of course there is the potential that any IP assets could grow in capital value dependant on the business growing.

There are a number of things that you and your professional administrator will want to consider before even starting to go through the process of getting any IP valued. This is yet again both of you undertaking the appropriate due diligence on such an investment. The things to consider, obtain or that you'll want to understand are likely to include:

- A business plan which will include the nature of the business, where the business is going and company accounts to show that it is a successful trading entity with forecasts for future growth.
- The formal structure of the business with regards to ownership and any share allocations.
- The length of time the business has been operating (the business is likely to have been operating for a numbers of years and at scale for it to be a viable investment).
- Details of the key competitors in relation to the business.
- An understanding of the brand strength, what the actual IP the business has is, and whether it is registered or unregistered.

Once you've reviewed and understood the above elements, it's only at this point you would even consider establishing any kind of valuation for the IP as this is where things start to get expensive.

Risks

Before we start to look at the costs involved, it's worth considering the risks of this kind of investment.

Whilst IP offers the potential for regular income and capital growth, it's also worth recognising there are serious hazards around this kind of investment for a pension. This is most certainly not suitable for an inexperienced investor/SSAS trustee. Although this is not a new asset area for possible pension investment, you need to be especially cautious and speak to suitably qualified advisors about any potential investments.

I think I would be on firm ground to say that many of you will not have heard that you can invest in IP using your SSAS, and even less of you will have done this. Equally I know of only a few SSAS professional administrators that will consider this type of investment.

The hoops that you will need to go through for this kind of investment, although not insurmountable, are significant. The SSAS trustees and administrators will have to fully satisfy themselves that this is a serious investment and worth its value.

As this kind of purchase is almost certainly to be a connected person transaction of some kind, it's important that a rigourous 'arms-length' valuation of the IP is obtained and fully documented should HMRC come knocking. At the same time, the business should only be paying market rates for the license fee it is paying. Any overpayment on either side could result in HMRC feeling that an unauthorised tax charge is appropriate…at least as far as they are concerned.

To obtain such a valuation it is important to use a suitably accredited firm and that firm is likely to be a specialist in the sector the business operates in. There is actually an ISO standard that deals with brand valuations specifically and this is ISO10668. This standard stipulates the approach that should be conducted in establishing the valuation for IP and includes things like the assumptions made, comparable IP valuations and how to go about the valuation.

The SSAS will also want to establish the future value of the investment as it will want to compare this to other options available in the market. It could be that, for whatever reason, the SSAS will want to sell this investment at some future date. If the only interested buyer is the company it is leasing the IP to, that could result in a lower future price.

Even worse, if the business has gone bust, who will now buy the IP that the SSAS is now holding? So again, it is really important the IP has some quantifiable value to be considered as a serious investment. We've previously mentioned liquidity of assets in this book and it's unlikely that any IP is going to be a liquid asset, so also consider this before there is any investment.

Now we understand that, what mistakes do business owners make about IP? Here's a list of some of the things that can leave gaping holes in the value of your IP:

1. You registered your trademark but didn't secure the URLs or social media profiles – if a competitor buys these, it can have a damaging effect. I see this all the time especially when people are in the process of starting a business or launching a product. They are so focused on getting it up and running and telling people what they are doing, they forget to register the business domain name. I actually saw a well-known author make this very mistake, announcing the name of his new book at a conference but I was amazed to see that he had not secured the domain name first! If there is one thing we've learnt from Covid-19, it's that you must have an online presence, so make sure you secure it.

2. The business name was never protected – just being registered at Companies House may not be enough to protect it. Registering a company gives you no rights other than to stop someone else registering the exact same name at Companies House.

3. It was assumed that since you made up a word or logo that you own it and trademark registration is unnecessary – well, wrong, even then you would need to trademark it to be fully protected.

4. A 'Do-It-Yourself' approach to IP - this often comes about because the owner sees little value in their IP. If you are a small business owner, it's easy to be too focused on running the business to consider such things but it may be

worthwhile engaging a specialist to protect it if you feel you have IP that has value.

5. Poor documentation - this can be a real problem for many business owners and is a natural extension of the DIY approach mentioned before.

6. Ignoring standard IP practices when focused on growing the business - where trademarks are concerned, at the very least, you need to ensure you have performed a trademark search to see if it is already being used by, or is similar to, that of another company.

7. Failing to implement appropriate confidentiality controls – this can be a recurring issue. Most businesses will use some form of non-disclosure agreement (NDA) when conducting their business, but online templates will often be weak in their protection. Outsourcing work (like coding) may also expose a business.

8. Finally, you did not create and implement an IP strategy – fail to plan, plan to fail, no more needs to be said.

These issues are real but they can be avoided if appropriate proactive due diligence steps are taken.

OK, enough of the business strategy work and back to the subject of this book.

Costs

I've already mentioned how specialised this kind of investment is and because of this, the costs associated with this approach are higher than many other areas of investment that are possible with a SSAS.

Equally those professional administrators that would consider this kind of investment as suitable for a SSAS, may have some set some financial criteria for approving such a loan. These may include:

- That the IP value needs to be in excess of a certain value e.g. in excess of £70,000-£100,000+

- That the SSAS can only lend a certain percentage of

the value of the SSAS e.g. 50% of its value (similar to a loanback), although up to 70% may be possible but 100% would almost certainly not be agreed.[31]

As a result of the above criteria, it is probable that only larger SSAS funds will be able to consider IP investments. This is probably a good filter, as larger funds are possibly more likely to have a larger business as their sponsoring employer, with a potentially suitable IP investment opportunity.

Finally

So, to wrap up this section on IP investment, investing in IP is clearly not for inexperienced pension trustees. It can be managed and utilised to add value to both the SSAS and the business involved for future growth. This can be of great value for connected parties who will share common objectives and have a belief in the strategy being employed by using the IP. That said, don't view this approach as an easy route to receive a cash injection for your business. Think very, very hard about the value of the investment in the sense that, if the worst-case scenario happened and the business folded, who is now going to buy the IP for a value at least as much as the SSAS paid for it? If no one is, maybe this investment is not right for the SSAS in this instance.

Investing in IP could potentially be a great enabler for your SSAS and the business, but speak to the specialised advisors if you are considering this type of investment.

Chapter 16

Renewable Energy

Now this is something I've become very interested in recently.

One of the positive things that did come about as a result of Covid-19 was the dramatic reduction in emissions – from factories, cars, power stations etc. Images shown on the news of normally polluted cities with now clear air above them was a game changer for me. It made me realise how quickly the pollution in the air can be improved if we switch away from fossil fuels to renewable energy. In the UK we also reached a major green milestone as, on the 10th June 2020, we went two whole months without starting up any coal fired power stations – this just happens to be the longest period since the industrial revolution.[32]

Now, most people find the subject of pensions rather difficult to comprehend, with their combination of technical complexity and the very long-term nature of most schemes. When you are young (in your 20's let's say), who really wants to think what life will be like when they are in their 50's, 60's, 70's......you get the idea. For most private investors, pension schemes are a real turn-off. This is unfortunate because the tax benefits with 100% income tax relief and exemption from capital gains tax are considerable.

I think the government is really missing a trick here with pensions and renewable energy. It seems to me that the investment opportunities which exist within this sector (particularly renewable energy) could be well suited to direct small pension investments with the right incentives. They are relatively long-term investments in nature and offer the opportunity for the underlying investments, especially in energy generation, to produce a regular income yield. If people (especially young people just setting up their pensions) can see there was a clear link between a pension investment and improving the environment with a positive impact on climate change (which the vast majority of people are concerned about), you must be on to a winner and would greatly improve people's engagement in pensions.

SSAS pensions (and SIPPs for that matter) would be a great vehicle that would allow pensions to invest in renewable energy or similar schemes in so many ways. They are not managed by large corporate houses that decide what the pension fund invests in, but by small groups of individuals with business experience who can consider the whole market approach to investing.

Of course, these areas are certainly not free of risk and because this is a relatively new sector for possible pension investment, you need to be especially cautious and speak to suitably qualified advisors about any potential investments. But people may be more comfortable with higher levels of risk if they can have a clearer understanding of the potential for returns, and this is what you generally get with a SSAS pension scheme as you are in control.

There are funds on the market that invest in renewable energy or other ethical investments. I am obviously not going to recommend anything here, but please do you own research and if this is of interest, this method of investment allows for a simple approach to invest into this market sector. If you want to invest directly into renewable energy, it is a little more involved as you'll see later in this chapter.

An Experts View of the Future

Now one of my favourite speakers about how the world will change over to renewable energy (solar to be specific is his opinion) is a guy called Tony Seba[33.]

I'm not going to go into detail here about what he predicts, but having a car industry background myself, it is truly game changing if some of his predictions come true. I highly recommend you watch some of the YouTube videos of public talks he has made, and listen to the changes he thinks are not that far away. I personally think it's just so interesting, and for me was a driver on why I included this section in this book. It should also be a reason why you should be considering this market sector for some of your SSAS investments. He certainly has inspired me to consider all things around renewable energy.

Renewable Energy as an Investment

Green energy is an area a lot of people are interested in from an investment point of view. There are several reasons why this is appealing. Firstly, many people genuinely care about issues like climate change and want to support businesses that are working to improve access to renewable energy and develop the technology in the sector. Secondly, it is a field where growth and technological advancements are very likely over the course of time, so seems well suited to longer term investment strategies like pension plans.

There are a number of things to consider when investing in renewable energy companies

Of course, the fact that renewable energy is on the rise and will replace current traditional fuels over the coming years and decades does not guarantee success for any one green energy focused company. If you want to focus your investment on renewable energy, be sure to do your research into how the companies you choose to invest in operate and what their near and long-term projections are.

Some green companies are less profit driven than others, which you may think of as a good thing in general but it isn't necessarily a good thing when it comes to investing your pension fund, but obviously that decision is down to you. You probably want to look to businesses that have stable operations and valuable assets (such as the land wind farms are based on, for example), don't make your portfolio too heavy on companies that spend a lot on R&D but don't generate much revenue. Such a company may have a 'break through', but the chances of you picking that particular company are remote to say the least. That said, it's still worth considering for some of your portfolio.

Look to Yield Generating Companies

There are different types of businesses in the green energy sector but what is called Yield Co's are often the most reliable when it comes to investment. Yield Co's are energy companies that run energy generating activities like solar, wind and hydropower installations. These are good since they already produce and sell energy and their expansion plans usually entail installing new installations, which they can manage and handle predictably without putting in too much risk.

The Forms of Renewable Energy Investment

Solar power is a sphere a lot of people have been investing in, however it is a highly competitive market and solar installations can be placed just about anywhere, meaning the assets a solar company owns are not usually as valuable as a wind farm or hydropower installation, which benefit from being in prime locations. Wind and hydropower can therefore be quite smart investments, though solar can still be wise if you pick a company with consistent performance and good business models.

I think renewable energy could be a great sector to invest in as part of your pension plan, however make sure you do your research into the choice of companies. Choose those likely to offer stable performance and survive an inevitable growth in competition. Remember to diversify your portfolio, even within the renewable energy sector, to reduce risk too.

Issues with Investing in Renewable Energy

Investing directly in wind and solar installations can be problematic. The issue with both is whether the structures fall within the definition of 'tangible moveable property' and therefore classed as taxable property.

The HMRC definition of tangible moveable property is things that can be touched and that are moveable rather than immovable property. The interpretation of this is that if the structure (wind farm, solar panels) are not integral within the land or building, it is by default moveable.

However, HMRC guidance confirms that there is no blanket classification for either, and so classification is determined on a case by case basis. Scheme providers and advisers like to deal with certainties and it comes as no surprise that this uncertainty presents both with a problem. For the majority of SSAS providers, the easy way to remove uncertainty is to say no to all such investments (not just in the case for renewable energy projects, but other types of investments as well), and this is what most of them do.

Wind Investment

Dealing with wind turbines first, how might HMRC view these structures? The substantial stand-alone structures seen on a wind farm (think about the many tall windfarms you see as you drive along major M roads in the UK) would probably be unlikely to be treated as tangible moveable property. Contrast this with a small turbine (maybe something only 10-foot-high placed at the rear of your premises), this is a very different structure and may be likely to trigger the charges associated with taxable property as a tangible moveable property. However, the size of the asset may not in itself be the determining factor, but if the wind turbine is significantly large (think of a structure the size of a tower block) and is as a matter of law fixed to the ground so as to become part of the land interest, then it could potentially not fall within the definition of tangible moveable property. Some SSAS administrators will now accept such structures as these into a pension scheme, even though the guidance from HMRC is unclear, but you need to be cautious and seek guidance from your suitably qualified advisors.

Another complication in this situation is the electricity that is generated by the turbine. If the scheme owns the land on which a large wind turbine is fixed and owns the turbine, if the electricity being generated by the wind turbine is also being sold back to the grid in some form, the scheme may be deemed to be trading. Income derived from trading is not investment income and therefore does not benefit from the tax breaks associated with such income. This, just to remind you, is not acceptable by HMRC and would result in a taxable charge which we need to avoid at all costs.

A potential way to get around the issue is for the SSAS not to own the wind turbine, but to lease the land to a third-party company (which we'll call Wind Co), so Wind Co buys the wind turbine to put on the land it is renting from the SSAS. In this situation, the Wind Co pays rent to the SSAS for using the land and Wind Co is the trading company. This means the SSAS is receiving allowable rent for use of its asset and is not trading.

Solar Investment

Let's now look at the case of solar panels. Where these are an integral part of the building and the pension scheme purchased the building and in doing so the solar panels as well, current HMRC guidance is that the panels would not be treated as tangible moveable property.

The problem in this situation is again the electricity. If any electricity generated by the panels ends up being sold back to the electrical utility network for a profit, then the SSAS could be considered to be trading.

Again, a potential way around this could be by leasing out the element that is generating the electricity. What I mean is that if the SSAS owned a commercial building and rented out the roof space to a Solar Co to install solar panels on it, we would have a situation that would be similar to the wind farm example above.

In theory, the trading of electricity would be done by the Solar Co, not the pension scheme, and in addition the rental income would be treated as tax efficient investment income of the pension scheme. It could be acceptable logic that the commercial building gets as much use of the electricity collected by the solar panels as it needs, with the surplus going to the Solar Co for it to sell to the grid, but you would need to check this with your professional advisors to see if this is acceptable.

Next Steps

Some of the above is based on logical assumptions and as we all know, to assume makes an 'ass' out of 'u' and 'me'. To really make SSAS pensions a driving force for renewable energy investments and engagement, we either need some real clarity from HMRC or from someone willing to make this a legal test case.

As you would expect, examples of using SSAS funds for renewable energy direct investments are quite thin on the ground at the moment, as this is still quite a new area for SSAS investments. Therefore, it is essential you run any such planned idea past your SSAS administrators first. There are clearly a number of obstacles to overcome, not least the potential tax implications, before making such an investment.

This route of SSAS direct investment into renewables is something I now plan to take up as a personal challenge as a result of writing this book. As I said at the start of this chapter, I think this is a missed opportunity by the UK government and I don't intend to let it go to waste…watch this space.

Chapter 17

Purpose

When I am educating myself on a subject, I try to gather as much information on the topic as I can. Not to the level an academic study would require, but to a sufficient level that I can either implement its use myself, or have an informed conversation on the subject with specialists in the field.

What started off as a data gathering and educational exercise quickly morphed into something that I felt other people would benefit from knowing. That is why I have found myself spending so much time pulling this book together.

One thing I have experienced in the property world is the willingness of so many people to help each other. There is a distinct lack of competitiveness between the majority of property investors as there is just so much opportunity out there. I think I can honestly say that, from all the property investors I have met, not one has only been out for themselves and damn everyone else. It makes for a very nice business community.

Having discovered the power of a SSAS pension, I felt this was something I had to share with people. On doing my research, I quickly found there was very little collated information that was in an understandable format. When you read documents from some SSAS administrator firms about the technicalities of investing with a SSAS, you sometimes feel they are trying to keep the details secret...almost as if they feel this is knowledge that mere mortals don't have the right to know about. To receive such life changing education, you must travel to the 'SSAS mountain' and pay homage to the 'SSAS gods' (and their fees of course) to be worthy of receiving such wisdom.

I exaggerate of course and not all professional SSAS administrators and accounting firms are like this, hopefully you have or will find a good one to work with.

A great saying I have tried to live by after hearing it is "What got you here, won't get you there." It's actually the title of a book by Marshall Goldsmith but I've seen the saying quoted in other books[34]. My personal interpretation of this saying is that you need to be constantly on an educational and learning journey – never, ever stop learning! This is something I try to live by everyday now and sometimes I amaze myself at the vast amount of relevant educational information I consume from books and podcasts.

Now having read this book, don't think you know everything you need to about a SSAS pension. Remember what I said at the beginning – I am not a financial advisor or qualified to give financial advice, so don't take anything I have written in this book as financial advice in any shape or form. Instead, use this book and its contents as a platform to go out and seek even more information on the subject.

Buy other authors' SSAS books (I will mention here a guy called Mark Stokes, as he was the first person I know of who wrote an understandable book on this subject), listen to property and finance podcasts (listening to 'The Property Voice' podcast by Richard Brown is how I first heard about this strange concept of investing in property using something called a SSAS), and of course, talk to a number of advisors on the subject. Consume as much as you feel you need to and start your SSAS investment process, but only if you feel it's right for you.

I hope you've found the contents informative if nothing else. After reading this you may feel it's not for you. Well, at least now you know. But maybe, just maybe, you do think this is something to consider. If I've been just a tiny part of the reason to set you on this path, then I would love it if you contacted me sometime in the future to tell me about the amazing investment deals you've done as a result of using a SSAS.

You can reach me through the following email address:

richard.parker@SSASpensionlegacy.co.uk

Who knows, when I update this book, maybe it will be one of your case studies that appears in these pages.

To finally conclude, I wish you every success on your SSAS investment journey and the legacy it will potentially leave behind you, whatever form that will be.

Chapter 18

References

1. Edmonds, C., 2003. Buffett: Expect 6%-7% Returns from the Market. TheStreet. [Online] Available at: <https://www.thestreet.com/opinion/buffett-expect-6-7-returns-from-the-market-10084972>

2. Her Majesty's Revenue and Customs (HMRC), 2015. Pensions Tax Manual. GOV.UK [Online] Available at: <https://www.gov.uk/hmrc-internal-manuals/pensions-tax-manual/ptm120000>

3. Webb, S., 2020. When will the earliest age you can tap into a pension rise to 57 - and should my wife use an Isa to bridge the gap? This Is Money [Online] Available at: <https://www.thisismoney.co.uk/money/pensions/article-7856699/When-does-minimum-age-cash-pension-rise-55-57.html>

4. Department of Finance, 2020. Lifetime Allowance for Tax Year 2020-21. [Online] Available at: <https://www.finance-ni.gov.uk/publications/lifetime-allowance-tax-year-2020-21>

5. Xafinity, 2019. Our SIPP vs SSAS. [Online] Available at: <https://www.xafinity.com/self-invested-pension/SIPP-vs-SSAS/Our-SIPP-vs-SSAS>

6. Investment Sense, 2012. Self-invested pensions: The comeback of the SSAS. [Online] Available at: <https://www.investmentsense.co.uk/self-invested-pensions-the-comeback-of-the-ssas/#more-18827>

7. Knight, A., 2018. Defined Benefit SSAS. Could this become your best kept secret? Rawanmoor. [Online] Available at: <https://rowanmoor.co.uk/insights/db-ssas-your-best-kept-secret/>

8. Gowling WLG International Limited, 2017. Legal Entity Identifier (LEI) Number – Does your pension need one? Available at: <https://gowlingwlg.com/en/insights-resources/articles/2017/legal-entity-identifier-lei-number-does-your-p/>

9. Brent Cru YCharts, n.d. Average Crude Oil Spot Proc: 39.46 USD/bbl for Jun 2020. [Online] Available at: <https://ycharts.com/indicators/average_crude_oil_spot_price>

10. Grand View Research (GVR), 2020. Report Overview. [Online] Available at: <https://www.grandviewresearch.com/industry-analysis/5g-services-market>

11. The Motley Fool, n.d. Stamp Duty On Shares [Online] Available at: <https://www.fool.co.uk/investing-basics/how-shares-are-taxed-2/stamp-duty-on-shares/>

12. Money Super Market, 2019. How the Financial Services Compensation Scheme protects your savings [Online] Available at: <https://www.moneysupermarket.com/savings/protecting-your-savings-guide/>

13. Landlord Vision, 2020. What Landlords Need to Know About Section 24 [Online] Available at: <https://www.landlordvision.co.uk/blog/section-24-landlord-guide/>

14. Penningtons Manches Cooper, n.d. FAQS - COMMERCIAL LEASES [Online] Available at: <https://www.penningtonslaw.com/expertise/business/real-estate/property-entrepreneurs/property-entrepreneurs-faqs/faqs-commercial-leases>

15. Roberts, A., and Mohindra, E., 2020. Stocks & Shares ISAs Find the best ISA or investment platform. Money Saving Expert [Online] Available at: <https://www.moneysavingexpert.com/savings/stocks-shares-isas/>

16. Goldstein, P., 2020. UK Hotel Capital Markets: Investment Review 2020. London: Knight Frank. [pdf] Available at: <https://content.knightfrank.com/research/1473/documents/en/uk-hotel-capital-markets-investment-review-2020-6957.pdf>

17. The World Tourism Organization (UNWTO) 2020. World Tourism Barometer Nº18 Juneuary 2020 [Online] Available at: <https://www.unwto.org/world-tourism-barometer-n18-Juneuary-2020>

18. Haywood, J., Mayock, P., Freitag, J., Akuffo Owoo, K., and Fiorilla, B., 2019. Airbnb & Hotel Performance: An analysis of proprietary data in 13 global markets. Hendersonville: STR. [Online] Available at: <https://str.com/sites/default/files/2019-07/Airbnb-and-Hotel-Performance.pdf>

19. GOV.UK. n.d. Stamp Duty Land Tax [Online] Available at: <https://www.gov.uk/stamp-duty-land-tax>

20. Knight Frank News, 2018. £1.32bn invested in UK healthcare real estate in 2017. Healthcare: Capital Markets [Online] Available at: <https://www.knightfrank.com/blog/2018/02/26/132bn-invested-in-uk-healthcare-real-estate-in-2017>

21. The Savills Blog, 2017. Care home investment: an increasingly attractive opportunity. [Online] Available at: <https://www.savills.co.uk/blog/article/218867/commercial-property/care-home-investment--an-increasingly-attractive-opportunity.aspx>

22. Office for National Statistics (ONS), 2019. National life tables, UK: 2016 to 2018 [Online] Available at: <https://www.ons.gov.uk/peoplepopulationandcommunity/birthsdeathsandmarriages/lifeexpectancies/bulletins/nationallifetablesunitedkingdom/2016to2018>

23. Hinrichs, E and Sparey, J., 2018. U.K. Care Homes: Is the Market Finally on the Brink of a New Wave of Investment? L.E.K. Consulting/Executive Insights, XX(41). [Online] Available at: <https://www.lek.com/insights/ei/uk-care-homes-market-brink-new-wave-investment>

24. Age UK, 2019. Later Life in the United Kingdom 2019. [pdf] Available at: <https://www.ageuk.org.uk/globalassets/age-uk/documents/reports-and-publications/later_life_uk_factsheet.pdf?dtrk=true>

25. Financial Conduct Authority (FCA), 2017. Land banking investment scams [Online] Available at: <https://www.fca.org.uk/scamsmart/land-banking-investment-scams>

26. Burges Salmon, 2019. Are the recent changes to Permitted Development rights welcome? [Online] Available at: <https://www.burges-salmon.com/news-and-insight/legal-updates/are-the-recent-changes-to-permitted-development-rights-welcome/>

27. Ward, A., 2020. Boris Johnson unveils "radical" planning reforms. Knight Frank [Online] Available at: <https://www.knightfrank.co.uk/research/article/2020-06-30-boris-johnson-unveils-radical-planning-reforms->

28. BBC News, 2020. Theo Paphitis: 'Retail will never, ever be the same again' [Online] Available at: <https://www.bbc.co.uk/news/av/business-52772056/theo-paphitis-retail-will-never-ever-be-the-same-again>

29. Music News, 2019. How much do Slade and The Pogues make at Christmas? [Online] Available at: <https://www.radiox.co.uk/news/music/how-much-do-slade-and-the-pogues-make-at-christmas/>

30. Truss, J., 2020. Top 5 Most Successful Businesses From Dragons' Den. Pocket Your Pounds [Online] Available at: <https://pocketyourpounds.co.uk/top-5-most-successful-businesses-from-dragons-den/>

31. Uren, A., 2013. As bank lending drought drags on, should entrepreneurs consider using their pension pot to invest in their business? This Is Money [Online] Available at: <https://www.thisismoney.co.uk/money/pensions/article-2352476/Pension-led-funding-entrepreneurs-consider-using-pension-fund-raise-finance.html>

32. Pavid, K., 2020. Britain goes two months without burning coal amid lockdown. Natural History Museum. [Online] Available at: <https://www.nhm.ac.uk/discover/news/2020/june/britain-goes-two-months-without-burning-coal.html>

33. Tony Seba, 2018. Clean Disruption of Energy and Transportation - CWA - Boulder, April 9, 2018. [Video Online] Available at: <https://www.youtube.com/watch?v=duWFnukFJh>

34. Goildsmith, M and Reiter, M., 2008. What Got You Here Won't Get You There: How Successful People Become Even More Successful. London: Profile Books

Printed in Great Britain
by Amazon

59179461R20098